Table of Contents

Supporting ESL Students
in Learning the Language of Mathematics

DR. JIM CUMMINS • UNIVERSITY OF TORONTO

Mathematics and Language

Mathematics can legitimately be considered to be a language in itself in that it employs symbols to represent concepts, symbols that facilitate our thinking about aspects of reality. However, mathematics is also intimately related to the natural language that we begin to acquire as infants, the language we use to communicate in a variety of everyday and academic contexts. Mathematics and language are interconnected at several levels:

• Teachers use natural language to explain mathematical concepts and perform mathematical operations. Students who have limited proficiency in English require additional support in order to understand mathematical concepts and operations taught in English. Among the supports that teachers can use to make instruction comprehensible for English language learners are demonstrations; concrete, hands-on manipulatives and graphic organizers; simplification and paraphrasing of instructional language; and direct teaching of key vocabulary.

• As is the case in other academic disciplines, mathematics uses a specialized technical vocabulary to represent concepts and, in the case of mathematics, describe operations. As early as Grade 1, students are required to learn the meanings of such words as *addition, subtraction, sum,* and *addend,* words that are likely to be found only in mathematics discourse. Furthermore, other terms have specific meanings in mathematics discourse that differ from their meanings in everyday usage and in other subject areas. Examples of these kinds of terms include words such as *table, product, even,* and *odd.* Homophones such as *sum* and *some* may also be confusing for ESL students. Grade 1 students are required to learn key concepts, such as *number facts* and *addition sentences,* at a time when many of them (ESL students, in particular) may not know the broader meanings of words such as *facts* and *sentences.*

• In addition to the technical vocabulary of mathematics, language intersects with mathematics at the broader level of general vocabulary, syntax, semantics, and discourse. Most mathematical problems require students to understand propositions and logical relations that are expressed through language. Consider this problem at the Grade 4 level:

> *Wendy gave a total of 10 treats to her dogs. She gave her large dog 2 more treats than she gave her small dog. How many treats did she give to each dog?*

Here students need to understand (or be able to figure out) the meanings of words such as *total* and *treats.* They need to understand the logical relation expressed by the *more … than …* construction. And they need to infer that Wendy has only two dogs, even though this fact is not explicitly included in the problem. Clearly, the language demands of the math curriculum increase as students progress through the grades, and these demands can cause particular difficulties for ESL students.

The ESL Challenge

Numerous research studies have demonstrated that ESL students generally require at least 5 years to catch up to native speakers in academic language proficiency (i.e., reading and writing skills; see Cummins, 2001 for a review). In mathematics, ESL students often make good progress in acquiring basic computation skills in the early grades. However, they typically experience greater difficulty in learning to interpret and solve word problems, and this difficulty increases in the later elementary grades as the word problems become more linguistically and conceptually complex.

These developmental patterns can be understood in relation to three very different aspects of language proficiency:

- **Conversational fluency** is the ability to carry on a conversation in familiar face-to-face situations. This is the kind of proficiency that the vast majority of native speakers of English have developed by the time they enter school at age 5. It involves the use of high-frequency words and simple grammatical constructions. ESL students generally develop basic fluency in conversational aspects of English within a year or two of exposure to the language, either within school or in their out-of-school environments.

- **Discrete language skills** reflect specific phonological, lexical, and grammatical knowledge that students can acquire in two ways: (a) as a result of direct instruction and (b) through both formal and informal practice (e.g., reading). Some of these discrete language skills are acquired early in schooling, and some continue to be acquired throughout schooling. The discrete language skills that are acquired early include knowledge of the letters of the alphabet, the sounds represented by individual letters and combinations of letters, and the ability to decode written words and pronounce them appropriately. ESL students can learn these specific language skills at a relatively early stage in their acquisition of English; in fact, these skills can be learned concurrently with their development of basic vocabulary and conversational proficiency.

  In mathematics, these discrete language skills include knowledge of the symbols that represent basic mathematical operations (e.g., + and −), the terms used to refer to these symbols and operations (*add, subtract, plus, minus,* etc.), and the basic technical vocabulary of mathematics. Clearly, the ability to decode written text is also a necessary (but not a sufficient) condition for thinking through and solving word problems expressed in written language.

- **Academic language proficiency** includes knowledge of the less frequent vocabulary of English as well as the ability to interpret and produce increasingly complex written language. As students progress through the grades, they encounter far more low-frequency words (primarily from Greek and Latin sources), complex syntax (e.g., the passive voice), and abstract expressions that are virtually never heard in everyday conversation. Students are required to understand linguistically and conceptually demanding texts in the content areas (e.g., literature, social studies, science, and mathematics) and to use this increasingly sophisticated language in accurate and coherent ways in their own writing.

Acquiring academic language proficiency is challenging for all students. Schools spend at least 12 years trying to extend the conversational language that native-speaking children bring to school into these more complex academic language spheres. It is hardly surprising, therefore, that research has repeatedly shown that ESL students usually require at least 5 years of exposure to academic English in order to catch up to native-speaker norms. In addition to internalizing increasingly complex academic language, ESL students must catch up to a moving target. Every year, native speakers are making large gains in their reading and writing abilities and in their knowledge of vocabulary. In order to catch up to grade norms within 6 years, ESL students must make 15 months' gain in every 10-month school year. By contrast, the typical native-speaking student is expected to make 10 months' gain in a 10-month school year (Collier & Thomas, 1999).

All three aspects of language proficiency are important. However, the three aspects—conversational fluency, discrete language skills, and academic language proficiency—are frequently confused by policy makers and by the media. For example, it is sometimes claimed that children acquire language rapidly and that one year of instructional support is sufficient to enable ESL students to catch up academically. In reality, many ESL students who have acquired fluent conversational skills are still a long way from grade-level performance in academic language proficiency (e.g., in reading comprehension in content areas such as math).

Similarly, the learning of discrete language skills does not generalize automatically to academic language proficiency. ESL (and native-speaking) students who can "read" a mathematical problem fluently may have only a very limited understanding of the words and sentences they can decode.

Thus, ESL students may require extended language support within the classroom in order to continue to make grade-level progress in content areas such as mathematics. Despite the fact that these students have acquired conversational fluency in English, together with basic mathematical vocabulary and computational skills, they may still experience gaps in their knowledge of some of the more sophisticated vocabulary, syntax, and discursive features of mathematical language.

Teaching the Language of Mathematics

From an instructional perspective, the relationship between language and mathematics is both two-way and reciprocal. Mathematical knowledge is developed through language, and language abilities can and should be developed through mathematics instruction. Specifically:

- Because mathematical concepts and operations are embedded in language, the specialized vocabulary of mathematics and the discursive features of mathematical propositions must be taught explicitly if students are to make strong academic progress in mathematics.

- Equally important, however, is the fact that in teaching mathematics, we are also developing and reinforcing students' general academic language proficiency. For example, think about the language learning that will likely occur as the teacher explains the following Grade 1 problem to a group of ESL students.

    Is 3 + 8 greater than 10, equal to 10, or less than 10? Explain.

Students will learn not only the specific meanings of the terms *greater than, equal to,* and *less than,* but also synonyms for these terms (e.g., a synonym for *great* is *big,* and the meaning of *greater than* is similar to the meaning of *bigger than*). This particular mathematics problem also presents the teacher an opportunity to teach students the general concept of *comparatives* and the general rule for forming comparatives (e.g., *great, greater, greatest; big, bigger, biggest*). The fact that not all comparatives take exactly these forms can also be taught in relation to *less, lesser, least.* Finally, the meaning of the word explain can be taught (e.g., *describe, tell about, tell why you think so*) and related to its use in other subject areas (e.g., science).

The reciprocal interdependence of language and mathematics becomes apparent, and even obvious, when perusing any mathematics textbook. Much of what students are expected to learn in mathematics is presented in written text. Students are required to read the text in order to develop their understanding of math concepts and their ability to solve math problems. Frequently, students are also required to explain orally or in writing how they solved a particular problem. Obviously, teachers and students will discuss these concepts; but without strong reading skills, students will find it very difficult to acquire, and truly assimilate, lesson content. Without strong writing skills, they will have difficulty demonstrating their knowledge of the concepts and skills that they are often, in fact, acquiring. Thus, effective reading and writing skills are necessary for students to make progress in mathematics, particularly as they move through the elementary grades. By the same token, the teaching of mathematics provides important opportunities for teachers to model academic language in their interactions with students and also to teach features of academic language directly (e.g., reading comprehension strategies, comparative adjectives, and context- or content-specific vocabulary).

Effective academic language instruction for ESL students across the curriculum is built on three fundamental pillars:

- **Activate Prior Knowledge/Build Background**
- **Access Content**
- **Extend Language**

In developing mathematical knowledge through language, and language abilities through mathematics, we can apply these three instructional principles in powerful ways.

Activate Prior Knowledge/Build Background

A. Prior knowledge as the foundation of learning

There is general agreement among cognitive psychologists that we learn by integrating new input into our existing cognitive structures or schemata. Our prior experience provides the foundation for interpreting new information. No learner is a blank slate. In fact, learning can be defined as the process of relating new information to the information we already possess. When we read a mathematical problem, for example, we construct meaning by bringing our prior knowledge of language, of mathematics, and of the world in general to the text. Our prior knowledge enables us to make inferences about the meanings of words and expressions that we may not have encountered before. As our prior knowledge expands through new learning, we are enabled to understand a greater range of mathematical concepts and also the language that expresses those concepts.

Thus, a major rationale for activating students' prior knowledge (or if there is minimal prior knowledge on a particular topic or issue, building it with students), is to make the learning process more efficient. It is important to *activate* students' prior knowledge because students may not explicitly realize what they know about a particular topic or issue; consequently, their prior knowledge may not facilitate learning unless it is brought to an immediate, and conscious, level.

B. Prior knowledge and ESL students

In a classroom that includes second-language learners from diverse backgrounds, prior knowledge about a particular topic may vary widely. Thus, simple transmission of certain information or a given skill will fail to connect with the prior knowledge and previous experience of many students. As a result, the input will be much less comprehensible for these students. Some students may have relevant information in their first language (L1), but not realize that there is any connection with what they are learning in English (L2). In other cases, the algorithms and strategies that students have acquired for carrying out math operations in their countries of origin may differ considerably from the procedures they are now being taught in English. Clearly, these discrepancies can cause confusion for students.

In teaching math to ESL students, it is important that we attempt to connect the instruction both with students' prior experience of learning math and with their prior knowledge of the world in general. In building up our own knowledge of students' educational and cultural backgrounds, we can collaborate with ESL teachers, who may have greater access to this information, and also with community volunteers, who can often provide invaluable insights about students' prior learning and cultural knowledge.

Lois Meyer (2000) has expressed clearly the importance of prior knowledge (familiarity with a given topic) in reducing the cognitive load of instruction for ESL students. She notes that the notion of *cognitive load* refers to the number and complexity of new concepts embedded in a particular lesson or text. This cognitive load depends not only on the text itself but also on the students' prior knowledge of the content.

> If the English learner has little entry knowledge about the subject matter, the cognitive load of the lesson will be heavy, for many concepts will be new and unfamiliar. The student will have little basis from which to generate hypotheses regarding the meanings the teacher is conveying through English.

> If the student's entry knowledge of the topic is considerable, this will lighten the cognitive load. Learners can draw on their knowledge to interpret linguistic and non-linguistic clues in the lesson in order to make educated guesses about the meanings of the teacher's talk and text (2000, p. 229).

Clearly, the cognitive load of many mathematical texts is considerable, particularly as students progress through the grades. Finding out what students know about a particular topic allows the teacher to supply relevant concepts or vocabulary that some or all students may be lacking, but which will be important for understanding the upcoming text or lesson. Building this context permits students to understand more complex language and to pursue more cognitively demanding activities. It lessens the cognitive load of the text and frees up students' brain power.

C. Strategies for Activating Prior Knowledge and Building Background

Three types of prior knowledge are relevant to consider in teaching mathematics: prior knowledge of math; knowledge that has been acquired through direct experiences; and knowledge acquired through secondary sources (e.g. books, videos, etc.). We can use brainstorming, role playing, and simulations, as well as connections to literature and other content areas to activate students' prior knowledge and build relevant background knowledge.

- **Connect to Prior Knowledge of Math** In Grade 1 we might activate students' knowledge of counting as a prelude to teaching them to use *counting on* as a tool for addition. Or at the Grade 4 level, we might activate students' knowledge of basic multiplication facts in order to reinforce the foundation for teaching more complex multiplication operations.

- **Connect to Prior Knowledge of Language** Although mathematics has its own technical language that students must learn, we explain this language, and the associated math operations, using more familiar everyday language. For example, in explaining the concept of *subtraction* we will use high frequency expressions such as *take away from* that are likely to be much more familiar to children. Typically, the meaning of this language will be reinforced through demonstrations involving concrete manipulatives or graphic organizers.

- **Connect to Prior Experiences** We can find out from students what activities they engage in outside of school and link mathematics instruction to those activities (e.g., students who engage in various sports can carry out a variety of operations relevant to those sports, such as calculating, comparing, and contrasting batting averages). We can also be proactive in *creating experiences* for students that will promote mathematical knowledge and skill. For example, we might engage parents as collaborators by having them work with their children in calculating the proportion of weekly food expenditures that the family spends on the various food groups, thereby reinforcing both social studies and math concepts.

- **Use Brainstorming, Role Playing, and Simulation** At a very early age most children develop an intuitive sense of "fairness" and an ability to judge whether goods of various kinds (e.g., toys or treats) have been distributed equally or fairly. We can use brainstorming, role-playing, and simulation to carry out a variety of math activities that tap into students' real-life experiences of equal (or fair) distribution. In the early grades, we would likely use concrete manipulatives to support these activities. In intermediate grades, real or simulated data can be used.

We can also link math to the development of critical thinking by having students carry out projects that go beyond the curriculum in various ways. For example, in a class with many ESL students we might have students brainstorm about the languages they know and how they learned them. On the basis of this brainstorming, they could then develop a questionnaire and carry out a more formal survey of the linguistic make-up of the class (or even the entire school). In analyzing data that reflect their own experiences and identities, students' motivation to explore effective analytic strategies and presentation tools (e.g., graphs and computerized slide shows) is likely to be considerably greater than when the activities are more distant from their experiences and interests.

- **Use Literature and Connections to Content** Relatively few people in North America have ever been in a jungle, but most adults and children can describe the main features of jungles as a result of secondary experiences of various sorts. In the classroom, we can use literature, high-interest expository texts, and other forms of media (e.g., videotapes) both to activate students' prior knowledge of math and also to build background knowledge.

  In some cases, connecting to prior experiences will involve use of stories that have been specifically selected because they contain relevant math content. In other cases, we will connect math concepts and operations to other subject matter across the curriculum. For example, we might link math to a social studies unit on government as we discuss where local and state governments get the funds to operate and as we have students calculate the sales taxes that their families pay for various kinds of purchases.

The essential point here is that the more connections we can make both to students' experiences and interests and to other areas of the curriculum, the more relevance math is likely to assume in students' minds and lives. This, in turn, will result in more powerful learning of math.

An additional consideration in activating ESL Students' prior knowledge is that this process communicates a sense of respect for what students already know and an interest in their cultural backgrounds. This affirmation of students' identities increases students' personal and academic confidence and motivates them to invest their identities more strongly in pursuing academic success.

Access Content

How can teachers make the complex language of mathematics comprehensible for students who are still in the process of learning English? How can students be enabled to take ownership of their learning of math concepts and operations rather than just learn rote procedures? One important strategy has already been noted in the previous section. Activating and building students' background knowledge is an essential part of the process of helping students to participate academically and gain access to meaning. When we activate students' prior knowledge we attempt to modify the "soil" so that the seeds of meaning can take root. However, we can also support or *scaffold* students' learning by modifying the input itself. We provide this scaffolding by embedding the content in a *richly redundant context* wherein there are multiple routes to the mathematical meaning at hand in addition to the language itself.

The following list presents a variety of ways of modifying the presentation of mathematical content to ESL students so that they can more effectively get access to the meaning in any given lesson.

- **Use Demonstration** Teachers can take students through a word problem in math, demonstrating step-by-step procedures and strategies in a clear and explicit manner.

- **Use Manipulatives (and Tools and Technology)** In the early grades manipulatives may include counters and blocks that enable students to carry out a mathematical operation, literally with their hands, and actually see the concrete results of that operation. At more advanced levels, measuring tools such as rulers and protractors and technological aids such as calculators and computers will be used. The effectiveness of these tools will be enhanced if they are used within the context of a project that students are intrinsically motivated to initiate and complete.

- **Use Small-Group Interactions and Peer Questioning** Working either as a whole class or in heterogeneous groups or pairs, students can engage in real-life or simulated projects that require application of a variety of mathematical skills. Díaz-Rico and Weed (2002) give as an example a project in which students are told that the classroom needs to be re-carpeted. They first estimate the area and then check their estimates with measuring tools. Working in groups, students could also calculate the potential cost of floor coverings using prices for various types of floor coverings obtained from local catalogues or advertisements.

- **Use Pictures, Real Objects, and Graphic Organizers** We commonly hear the expression "A picture is worth a thousand words." There is a lot of truth to this when it comes to teaching academic content. Visuals enable students to "see" the basic concept we are trying to teach much more effectively than if we rely only on words. Once students grasp the concept, they are much more likely to be able to figure out the meanings of the words we use to talk about it. Among the visuals we can use in presenting math content are these: *pictures/photographs, real objects, graphic organizers, drawings on overhead projectors,* and *blackline masters.* Graphic organizers are particularly useful because they can be used not only by teachers to present concepts but also by students to take notes, organize their ideas in logical categories, and summarize the results of group brainstorming on particular issues. Some graphic organizers that are useful for teaching math are *Venn diagrams; pie and bar graphs; K-W-L charts* (What we know, what we want to know, and what we have learned; *T-charts* (e.g., for comparing and contrasting); *Problem and Solution charts; Main Idea and Details charts; Cause and Effect charts; Sequence charts;* and *Time Lines.*

- **Clarify Language (Paraphrase Ideas, Enunciate Clearly, Adjust Speech Rate, and Simplify Sentences)** This category includes a variety of strategies and language-oriented activities that clarify the meanings of new words and concepts. Teachers can modify their language to students by *paraphrasing ideas and by explaining new concepts and words.* They can explain new words by providing synonyms, antonyms, and definitions either in English or in the home language of students, if they know it. Important vocabulary can be repeated and recycled as part of the paraphrasing of ideas. Teachers should speak in a natural rhythm, but enunciate clearly and adjust their speech to a rate that ESL students will find easier to understand. Meaning can also be communicated and/or reinforced through gestures, body language, and demonstrations.

Because of their common roots in Latin and Greek, much of the technical math vocabulary in English has cognates in Romance languages, such as Spanish (e.g., *addition—adición*). Students who know these languages can be encouraged to make these cross-linguistic linkages as a means of reinforcing the concept. Bilingual and English-only dictionaries can also be useful tools for language clarification, particularly for intermediate-grade students.

- **Use Total Physical Response, Gestures, and Pantomime** For beginning ESL Students, *Total Physical Response,* activities wherein students act out commands, can be highly effective. Math calculations can be embedded in the commands that students act out. For example, students can progress from fully acting out the command "Take 5 steps forward and then 2 steps backward" to calculating in their heads that they need take only 3 steps forward to reach the destination. Additionally, the meanings of individual words can be demonstrated through *gestures* and *pantomime.*

- **Give Frequent Feedback and Expand Student Responses** *Giving frequent feedback* means responding positively and naturally to all forms of responses. Teachers can let their students know how they are doing by responding to both their words and their actions. Teachers can also assess their students' understanding by asking them to give examples, or by asking them how they would explain a concept or idea to someone else. *Expanding student responses* often means using polar (either/or) questions with students who are just beginning to produce oral English and "wh" (who, what, when, where, why) questions with students who are more fluent. Teachers can easily, and casually, expand their students' one- and two-word answers into complete sentences ("Yes, a triangle does have three sides") and respond to grammatically incorrect answers by recasting them using standard English syntax (Student: "I gotted 4 tens and 1 one"; Teacher: "That's right, you have 4 tens and 1 one").

Extend Language

A systematic focus on and exploration of language is essential if students are to develop knowledge of the specific vocabulary and discursive patterns within the genre of mathematical language. As noted above, investigation of the language of mathematics can also develop in students a curiosity about language and deepen their understanding of how words work. Three strategies for extending students' knowledge of the language of mathematics are outlined below.

A. Creating mathematical language banks
Students can systematically collect the meanings of words and phrases they encounter in mathematical texts in a personal or group *language bank.* Ideally, the language bank would be created in a series of files within the classroom computer but it can also be done with paper and pencil in a class notebook.

Paradoxically, the complexity of mathematical language provides some important opportunities for language exploration. As mentioned above, a large percentage of the less frequent academic and technical vocabulary of English derives from Latin and Greek roots. One implication of this is that word formation follows some very predictable patterns. These patterns are similar in English and Spanish.

When students know some of the rules or conventions of how academic words are formed, it gives them an edge in extending their vocabulary. It helps them figure out not only the meanings of individual words but also how to form different parts of speech from those words.

A central aspect of academic language is *nominalization*. This refers to the process whereby abstract nouns are formed from verbs and adjectives. Take, for example, four common verbs that occur in the math curriculum: *multiply, divide, measure,* and *equal.* The word families (excluding verb forms and plurals) for each of these words are presented below.

Verb	Noun	Adjective
multiply	multiplication multiple multiplicity	multiple
divide	division dividend	divisive divided
measure	measure measurement	measured
equal equalize	equality equal equalizer	equal equitable

We see in these four word families, several common ways in which the English language forms nouns from verbs. One pattern is to add the suffix *-tion* or *-ion* to the verb form as in *multiplication, division,* and many other mathematical terms, such as *estimation, notation,* and *operation.* Another pattern is to add the suffix *-ment* as in *measurement,* while a third pattern is to add the suffix *-ity* or *-ty* as in *equality, capacity, property,* and *probability.* When we demystify how this academic language works, students are more likely to recognize parts of speech in their reading of complex texts across the curriculum and to become more adept at inferring meaning from context. For example, when a student recognizes that *acceleration* is a noun (rather than a verb or an adjective), he or she is one step closer to understanding the meaning of the term in the context of a particular sentence or text.

Students can be encouraged to use dictionaries (in both English and their L1, when available) to explore the more subtle meanings of these mathematical words. For example, students could be asked to work in pairs or small groups to think through the differences in meaning between the verbs *equal* and *equalize;* among the nouns *equality, equal,* and *equalizer;* and between the adjectives *equal* and *equitable.*

This nominalization process also permits us to think in terms of abstract realities or states and to use higher-level cognitive functions that require uses of language very different from the conversational or "playground" language that we acquire in everyday situations. This point is made clearly by Pauline Gibbons:

> The playground situation does not normally offer children the opportunity to use such language as: *if we increase the angle by 5 degrees, we could cut the circumference into equal parts.* Nor does it normally require the language associated with the higher-order thinking skills, such as hypothesizing, evaluating, inferring, generalizing, predicting, or classifying. Yet these are the language functions which are related to learning and the development of cognition; they occur in all areas of the curriculum, and without them a child's potential in academic areas cannot be realized (1991, p. 3).

Gibbons goes on to point out that explicit modeling of academic language is particularly important in schools with large numbers of ESL students:

> In such a school it is very easy to fall into the habit of constantly simplifying our language because we expect not to be understood. But if we only ever use basic language such as *put in* or *take out* or *go faster,* some children will not have any opportunity to learn other ways of expressing these ideas, such as *insert* or *remove* or *accelerate.* And these are the words that are needed to refer to the general concepts related to the ideas, such as *removal, insertion,* and *acceleration* (1991, p. 18).

In short, when students know some of the rules or conventions of how academic words are formed, it gives them an edge in extending their vocabulary. It helps them figure out not only the meanings of individual words but also how to form different parts of speech from these words. One way of organizing students' language detective work in mathematics is to focus separately on *meaning, form,* and *use.* Working in pairs or small groups, students can be encouraged to collect and explore one mathematics word per day, focusing on one or more of these three categories.

- **Focus on Meaning** Categories that can be explored within a Focus on Meaning include *Mathematical meaning; Everyday meaning; Meaning in other subject areas; L1 equivalents; Related words in L1 (cognates); Synonyms; Antonyms; Homonyms; Meaning of prefix; Meaning of root;* and *Meaning of suffix.* Not all of these categories will be relevant for every word, but considered together they provide a map of directions that an exploration of meaning might pursue. Take a possible exploration of the word *subtract:*

Mathematical meaning:	take one number or quantity from another (or compare two numbers or quantities)
L1 equivalent (Spanish):	restar, sustraer
Synonym:	deduct
Antonym:	add
Meaning of prefix:	under or away
Meaning of root:	from the Latin for "pull"

- **Focus on Form** Most of the root words in mathematics that come from Latin and Greek form not just one part of speech; we can make nouns, verbs, and adjectives from many of these root words. If we know the typical patterns for forming nouns and adjectives from root verbs, we can recognize these parts of speech when they appear in text. The implications for expanding students' vocabulary are clear: rather than learning just one word in isolation, students are enabled to learn entire *word families,* a process that can dramatically expand their working vocabulary.

  Categories that can be explored within a Focus on Form include *Word family and grammatical patterns; Words with the same prefix; Words with the same root;* and *Words with the same suffix.* Consider again the word *subtract:*

Word family/ grammatical patterns:	subtract, subtracts, subtracted, subtracting (verb forms)
	subtraction, subtractions (noun forms)
Words with same prefix:	substitute, subtotal, suburban, subway
Words with same root:	tractor, traction

- **Focus on Use** Students can explore the range of uses of particular words through brainstorming as a class or small group; looking words up in dictionaries, encyclopedias, or thesauri; or asking parents or other adults outside of school. Categories that can be explored within a Focus on Use include *General uses; Idioms; Metaphorical uses; Proverbs; Advertisements; Puns;* and *Jokes.* For the word *subtract,* most students will not find much that will fall within these categories other than the category of *general uses.* However, with some of the more frequent words in mathematical discourse that derive from the Anglo-Saxon lexicon of English rather than the Greek/Latin lexicon, many of these other categories will yield a multitude of examples. Consider the multiple meanings and figurative uses of words such as *great* (as in "greater than"), *big,* and *double* that students might explore.

  In short, when students explore the language of mathematics by collecting specimens of mathematical language in a systematic and cumulative way, they expand not only their understanding of mathematical terms and concepts but also their knowledge of how the English language works (e.g., the fact that abstract nouns are often formed in English by adding the suffix *-tion* to the verb). The development of language awareness in this way will benefit students' reading comprehension and writing ability across the curriculum.

B. Taking ownership of mathematical language by means of "reporting back"

If students are to take ownership of mathematical language, we must provide ample opportunities and encouragement for them to use this language for authentic purposes in the classroom. In the absence of active use of the language, students' grasp of the mathematical register is likely to remain shallow and passive.

Researchers (e.g., Swain, 1997) have noted three ways in which L2 acquisition is stimulated by active use of the language:

- Students must try to figure out sophisticated aspects of the target language in order to express what they want to communicate.

- It highlights to both students and teachers the aspects of language the students still find troublesome.

- It provides teachers with the opportunity to provide corrective feedback to build language awareness and help students figure out how the language works.

- **Have Students Report Back Orally and in Writing** One example of how this process operates in the teaching of content areas such as mathematics is provided by Gibbons (1991). She emphasizes the importance of *reporting back* as a strategy for promoting academic language development. For example, after a concrete, hands-on group experience or project, students are asked to report back to the class orally about what they did and observed and then to write about it. As students progress from concrete, hands-on experience to more abstract oral and written language use, they must include sufficient information within the language itself for the meaning to be understood by those who did not share in the original experience. She notes that

> while hands-on experiences are a very valuable starting point for language development, they do not, on their own, offer children adequate opportunities to develop the more 'context-free' language associated with reading and writing....
> [A] reporting-back situation is a bridge into the more formal demands of literacy. It allows children to try out in speech—in a realistic and authentic situation—the sort of language they meet in books and which they need to develop in their writing. Where children's own language background has not led to this extension of oral language, it becomes even more important for the classroom to provide such opportunities (1991, p. 31).

In short, students become more aware of the cognitive processes and strategies they use to solve math problems, and they are enabled to take ownership of the language that reflects and facilitates these cognitive processes, when the curriculum provides extensive opportunities for them to explain orally and in written form what they did and how they did it.

C. Mastering the language of mathematical assessment

- **Have Students Create Test Items** High-stakes testing has become a fact of life in classrooms across the United States, and consequently a large majority of curriculum materials include not only formative assessment integrated within the curriculum unit but also practice oriented to performance on state-wide standardized tests. Consistent with the emphasis on providing opportunities for students to take ownership of the language of mathematics through active use of that language, we can also encourage students to gain insight and control over the language of mathematical assessment. We can do this by having students create their own multiple-choice (or other relevant) tests in mathematics rather than always being on the receiving end of tests that adults have created. The process might work as follows.

In order to familiarize students with the process (and also have some fun in a friendly, competitive context), we can have them work in heterogeneous groups to construct their own tests, initially on topics with which they are familiar or on which they have carried out research. For example, the teacher might explain how multiple-choice items are constructed (e.g., the role of distractors), and each group might construct a set of approximately 5 items on topics such as baseball, popular music, television programs, or popular slang. These items are then pooled and the entire set of items is administered as a test to the entire class. Subsequently, each group might research aspects of a particular content area and construct items based on their research. In the context of math, groups could construct test items that focus on the unit of study (e.g., fractions or decimals) that has just been completed. An incentive system could be instituted such that the groups gain points based on their performance on the pooled test that leads ultimately to some reward.

The rationale for this reversal of roles is that construction of test items is more cognitively challenging (and engaging) than simply responding to test items. In order to come up with items that will be challenging for the other groups, students must know the content of the unit in an active rather than a passive way. The within-group discussion and collaboration in generating the items and distractors is also likely to reinforce both language and content knowledge for all students in the group, but particularly for those students (likely including some ESL students) whose grasp of the content may be fragile.

Within this conception, standardized math tests are viewed as one particular genre of math language. Students should be familiar with the conventions of this genre if their academic worth is to be recognized. In generating multiple-choice test items, students are developing language awareness in the context of a highly challenging (but engaging) cognitive activity.

The same principle can be applied to the creation of other forms of assessment that tap both math and language concepts. For example, teachers could have students create multiple-choice cloze sentences that reflect both everyday and math-specific meanings of mathematical vocabulary.

1. Five _____ six _____ eleven.
2. On the _____ side, my share _____ his.
3. On the _____ side, his share is _____ mine.
4. Numbers less than zero are called _____ numbers.
5. When we multiply by two, we _____ the quantity.

Target Words
plus
double
equals
negative

Conclusion

Mathematics will assume relevance to students and be learned much more effectively when they can relate the content to their prior experience and current interests. In addition to activating students' prior knowledge and building background, we may need to modify our instruction in specific ways to make the content accessible to ESL students who are still in the process of catching up to native speakers in academic English- language proficiency. This catch-up process will typically take at least 5 years, partly because students are catching up to a moving target—native speakers of English are not standing still, waiting for ESL students to bridge the gap. Thus, even ESL students who are relatively fluent in English may require specific support in accessing mathematical concepts and problems expressed in English.

These supports should focus not only on making the mathematics content comprehensible to students but also on extending their awareness of how the language of mathematics works. In this way, students can develop insights about academic language that will bear fruit in other content areas (e.g., reading comprehension in language arts and vocabulary building in social studies). A goal of this process of extending students' command of academic language is to enable them to take ownership of the language of the curriculum and use it for authentic purposes. Thus, they will benefit from opportunities to carry out projects and explain what they did both orally and in written form. As the audience becomes more distant (e.g., in the case of a more formal written report), students are required to use more abstract, explicit, and precise language to communicate their meaning. When we integrate these active uses of language with the mathematics curriculum, students benefit both with respect to mathematics and to language facility.

References

Collier, V. P. and Thomas, W. P. (1999). Making U.S. schools effective for English language learners, Part 1. *TESOL Matters,* 9:4 (August/September), pp. 1 & 6.

Cummins (2001). *Negotiating identities: Education for empowerment in a diverse society.* 2nd edition. Los Angeles: California Association for Bilingual Education.

Díaz-Rico, L. & Weed, K. Z. (2002). *The crosscultural, language, and academic development handbook: A complete K–12 reference guide.* 2nd edition. Boston: Allyn & Bacon.

Gibbons, P. (1991). *Learning to learn in a second language.* Newtown, Australia: Primary English Teaching Association.

Meyer, L. (2000). Barriers to meaningful instruction for English learners. *Theory into Practice,* 34(2), 228–236.

Swain, M. (1997). Collaborative dialogue: Its contribution to second language learning. *Revista Canaria de Estudios Ingleses,* 34, 115–132.

Inside and Outside

ACCESS CONTENT; ACTIVATE PRIOR KNOWLEDGE/BUILD BACKGROUND

Objective Use the words *inside* and *outside* to describe the position of objects.

Materials Apron or jacket with large pockets (optional); everyday items such as a pencil and a small book

Vocabulary Inside (in), outside (out)

ESL Strategies   *Use before*   **LEARN**   ⏱ 10 MIN

Use ➤ Demonstration
If possible, wear an apron or jacket with large pockets for this activity. In one pocket, place an everyday item such as a pencil. Then place another item, such as a small book, on a table or desktop. Lift the pencil out of your pocket, point to it, and then put it back in your pocket. **Where is the pencil? The pencil is <u>inside</u> my pocket.** Point to the book. **Is the book inside my pocket? No, the book is <u>outside</u> my pocket.** Take the pencil out of your pocket and ask: **Where is the pencil now?** Prompt children to say that the pencil is outside your pocket.

Repeat the activity, using different items. As each item is placed in an "inside" or "outside" position, ask who can tell where the item is. (If a child is not yet ready to produce a complete sentence, encourage him or her to say the appropriate positional word, perhaps while using an accompanying gesture.)

Use ➤ Brainstorming
Create a two-column chart on the board. Label the columns "Inside" and "Outside." Have children brainstorm a list of things inside the classroom, such as books, chairs, and children, and a list of things outside the classroom, such as the playground, trees, the parking lot. Write children's ideas in the appropriate columns and encourage them to use *inside* or *outside* to describe the location of each thing or person named as you record the name on the chart.

Over, Under, and On

ACCESS CONTENT; EXTEND LANGUAGE

Objective Use the words *over, under,* and *on* to describe the position of objects.

Materials 1 large item that is easy to see, such as a beachball or a building block

Vocabulary Over (above), under (below), on (on top of)

ESL Strategies   *Use before*   **LEARN**   ⏱ 10–15 MIN

Use ➤ Demonstration
Place a chair in front of the room so everyone can see it. Ask a volunteer to sit in the chair. Hold up a colorful item, such as a beachball, that is easy for everyone to see. Hold it <u>over</u> the child's head. **The ball is over (Child's) head.**

Have children repeat the sentence with you as they are able. Place the ball _under_ the chair where the child is sitting. **Now the ball is under (Child's) chair.** Have children repeat the sentence with you as they are able. Place the ball _on_ the child's lap. **Now the ball is on (Child's) lap.** Again, have children repeat the sentence as they are able. Then go through each step again, this time having children answer questions about the ball's location: **Where is the ball?** _(Over [Child's] head)_ Continue, using _under_ and _on_.

Focus on Meaning ➤ Divide the class into pairs. Have each pair of children choose their own object and repeat the steps. One child sits in a chair while the other child positions the object, in any order, _over_ the seated child's head, _under_ the seated child's chair, and _on_ the seated child's lap. The child who is seated should, if possible, use a sentence to tell where the item is. (If a child is not yet ready to produce a complete sentence, encourage him or her to say the appropriate positional word: _over, under,_ or _on._) Children then change places and repeat the activity.

Top, Middle, and Bottom

EXTEND LANGUAGE; ACTIVATE PRIOR KNOWLEDGE/BUILD BACKGROUND

USE WITH LESSON 1-3

Objective Use the words _top, middle,_ and _bottom_ to describe position.

Materials Empty 3-shelf bookcase (or 3 stacked empty crates or boxes); box filled with classroom toys, such as toy cars and blocks; _(per child)_ 1 two-color counter.

Vocabulary Top, middle (between), bottom

ESL Strategies

Use before **LEARN**

🕐 10–15 MIN

Focus on Meaning ➤ Play a game with children to help them review the meanings of the words _top, middle,_ and _bottom._ Place a counter on the top shelf of an empty bookcase and use gestures as you say: **The counter is on the top shelf.** Encourage children to repeat the model sentence after you as they are able. Then invite each child, one at a time, to place his or her counter on the top shelf. **Where is the top shelf?** Have children point to it. **The top shelf is where the counter is. The middle and bottom shelves don't have any counters on them. Who would like to move the counter from the top shelf to the middle shelf?** Choose a volunteer. **Who would like to move the counter from the middle shelf to the bottom shelf?** Choose a volunteer. Encourage children to use positional vocabulary as they move the counter from one shelf to another. Then, as time allows, choose children to "play teacher": they choose a classmate and give him or her directions about where to place the counter.

Use Role Playing ➤ Bring out the box filled with classroom toys. Place one or two of them randomly on each shelf. Have one volunteer pretend to be a clerk in a toy store. Invite another child to be a customer in the store. Have the customer greet the clerk and ask about the price of a particular toy by identifying its position on a particular shelf: "I'd like to see the red car on the middle shelf. How much does it cost?" Invite the clerk to respond: "Here it is. It costs $2.00." Have pairs of children continue the role play and lead the class in comparing and contrasting the words *top, middle,* and *bottom* in relation to the locations of given toys.

Left and Right

USE WITH LESSON 1-4

ACTIVATE PRIOR KNOWLEDGE/BUILD BACKGROUND; ACCESS CONTENT

Objective Use the words *left* and *right* to describe position.

Materials *(per child)* 1 sheet of construction paper; crayons; construction-paper bracelet (made from one strip with the ends taped together)

Vocabulary Left, right

ESL Strategies   *Use before* **CHECK** ✓   🕐 15–20 MIN

Connect to Prior Knowledge of Language ➤ Give each child a sheet of construction paper. Tell children they will make hand tracings. **First, raise your <u>right</u> hand.** Make sure all children are showing the correct hand. Then have each child place his or her right hand on the construction paper and make a tracing. Then have children repeat the process using their <u>left</u> hands. Continue to reinforce the meanings of *right* and *left* as children work. Encourage them to use the words, too.

Use Total Physical Response ➤ Have children sit in a circle. Give each of them a construction-paper bracelet. Reinforce the positional meaning of the word *right* as you help children put the bracelets on their right arms. Then lead them in a game of Simon Says. **Simon says put your right hand on your head.**

Help children understand how to perform the command. Explain that in Simon Says, a command that begins with "Simon says …" must be obeyed. But anyone who performs an action when Simon hasn't said to do it is "out."

Simon says put your right hand on your left foot. Check to make sure that all children are performing the action correctly. **Now put your left hand on your right foot.** (Pause.) **Uh-oh! Simon didn't say to do that, did he? So if you did it, you have to go back to your chair and sit down.** (Allow time for children who are "out" to return to their seats.) **Simon says put your left hand on your nose.** Continue the game, sometimes saying "Simon says," sometimes not. The winner is the last child left in the circle.

Same and Different

USE WITH LESSON 1-5

ACCESS CONTENT

Objective Identify *same* and *different* by the attributes of color, shape, size, and kind.

Materials 1 red and 1 green, same-sized construction-paper circles; 2 yellow, different-sized construction-paper triangles; *(per group)* pair of similar items: a magazine and a hardcover book, a pencil and a pen, a penny and a tennis ball, and so on

Vocabulary Same (alike), different

ESL Strategies *Use before* **LEARN** ⏱ 10–15 MIN

Use Demonstration ➤ Hold the same-sized red and green circles up so children can see them. **How are these two shapes the <u>same</u>?** Prompt children to recognize that they are both circles and are the same size. **How are they <u>different</u>?** Prompt children to recognize that they are different in color.

Hold up the different-sized yellow triangles. **How are these two shapes the same?** *(They are both yellow, and they are both triangles.)* **How are they different?** *(They are different sizes. One is bigger and one is smaller.)*

Use Small-Group Interactions ➤ Divide the class into small groups. Then hand out a pair of similar items, such as a magazine and a book, to each group. Have a volunteer lead each group in asking: "How are these two things the same? How are they different?" Have other children in the group answer the questions. Circulate among the groups and ask clarifying questions as necessary, referring to various attributes the objects may or may not have in common. *(For example, the magazine and the book are both made of paper. But the magazine has a soft cover, and the book has a hard cover.)*

Sorting by One Attribute

USE WITH LESSON 1-6

ACCESS CONTENT

Objective Sort objects by one attribute, such as color, shape, size, or kind.

Materials Circles, triangles, squares, and rectangles cut out of red, yellow, and blue construction paper

Vocabulary Sort

Use before LEARN

Use Manipulatives ➤ Hold up a red circle. **What shape is this?** *(A circle)* Hold up a yellow circle. **What shape is this?** *(A circle)* **That's right, they are both circles. They have the same shape.** With your finger, slowly trace the outline of each circle. Repeat this process with construction-paper triangles, rectangles, and squares.

Stand two red circles and one red triangle in the chalk tray so that they are displayed against the board. **Who can help me <u>sort</u> these three shapes by finding the two that are the same?** As a child holds up the two red circles say: **Yes, these two shapes are the same. What makes them the same?** *(They are both round; they are both circles.)*

Stand two circles and one triangle, each a different color, in the chalk tray. **Who can help me sort these three shapes by finding the two that are the same?** As a child holds up the two different-colored circles, say: **Yes, these two shapes are the same. Is it the color that makes them the same?** *(No, they are different colors. It is the shape that makes them the same.)*

Repeat for triangles, rectangles, and squares, occasionally sorting by another attribute, such as color or size.

Sorting the Same Set in Different Ways

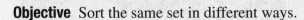

ACCESS CONTENT

Objective Sort the same set in different ways.

Materials Basket or bucket filled with balls of different sizes and colors (but all the same shape: round), such as tennis balls, golf balls, handballs, soccer balls

Use before LEARN

Use Real Objects ➤ Show children the basket filled with balls of different sizes and colors (and patterns). **As you can see, I have many balls in this basket. How are these balls all the same?** *(They are all round.)* Hold up one of the balls and slowly move your fingers around the spherical shape of the ball. **All of these balls are round. So all of these balls have the same shape. It is their shape that makes them the same.**

Show children the basket again and ask them to take another look. **We see that all of these balls have the same shape. They are all round. But do all of these balls look exactly the same?** Take a few out and line them up on the chalk tray. **In some ways these balls are different from one another. This means that in some ways these balls are not the same. Who knows one way in which these balls are different from one another?** *(They are different sizes.)* **Who knows another way in which these balls are different from one another?** *(They are different colors. Some of them have patterns.)* If a child suggests an incorrect answer, let the child explain his or her answer and give the child the opportunity to suggest another answer.

Since the balls are different sizes, we can sort them by size. We can put all of the small balls together. And we can put all of the larger balls together. I will begin sorting the balls by size. Rearrange some of the balls in the chalk tray so they are sorted by size: **Who would like to help me finish sorting these balls by size?**

As time allows, have children work together to sort the balls by color.

Sorting by More Than One Attribute

USE WITH LESSON

1-8

ACTIVATE PRIOR KNOWLEDGE/BUILD BACKGROUND; EXTEND LANGUAGE

Objective Use more than one attribute to sort a set of objects.

Materials Square toy blocks of various sizes

ESL Strategies

Use before LEARN

⏱ 10 MIN

Connect to Prior ➤ Knowledge of Math

Remind children that they have already learned how to sort things that are alike. **We know that some things are alike in one way. Now we are going to see how some things can be alike in more than one way.** Place several toy blocks in front of the children. **Who can tell me how these blocks are alike?** Give children time to consider common characteristics. **Yes, they are all square. They are all the same in that way.** Invite children to notice other ways in which some of the blocks are the same. Children may notice that some of the blocks are the same in color, size, or pattern.

How are some of these blocks different? Children may notice that some blocks are different in size or color. **Can you think of a way that some of these blocks are alike?** Prompt children to see that some blocks are big and some are small. **First I am going to sort these blocks by size. I will put the small blocks in one pile and the big blocks in another pile.** Ask children to help you as you work. **Have we correctly sorted all of the blocks by size?** Test the children's understanding by placing a very small block in the big-block pile, and a big block in the small-block pile and then asking: **Is this correct?** Review the sorting rule.

Problem-Solving Strategy: Use Logical Reasoning

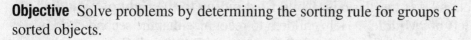

USE WITH LESSON
1-9

ACCESS CONTENT

Objective Solve problems by determining the sorting rule for groups of sorted objects.

Materials *(per group)* Pictures cut from magazines of several items in each of various categories, such as children, food, and animals; masking tape

Vocabulary Sorting rule

ESL Strategies

Use before LEARN

🕐 10–15 MIN

Use Pictures ➤ Tape four pictures cut from magazines on the board. Make sure they share a similar detail or theme, such as what the person in each picture is doing (perhaps playing a sport). **Why do you think I grouped these four pictures together?** Guide children to notice details about each picture. **In the first picture, the boy is wearing a bicycle helmet. In the second picture, the girl is wearing a baseball cap. In the third picture, the man is wearing a sun visor.** Guide children to observe what makes these three pictures similar. **That's right: the people in these three pictures are all wearing hats.**

But now let's look at the last picture. In the last picture, the woman is not wearing a hat. She's playing tennis, but she's not wearing a hat. So not all of these pictures are of people wearing hats. And that means that "people wearing hats" is not the reason these four pictures are grouped together. "People wearing hats" is not our <u>sorting rule</u>. What do you think the sorting rule is? You will probably need to explain that a sorting rule is the way in which things are grouped together. Give children several minutes to think about what the sorting rule is for this group of four pictures. Ask for volunteers to suggest what the rule is until you arrive at the right rule. **That's right, all of these pictures show people playing sports.**

Use Small-Group ➤
Interactions Divide the class into small groups. Hand out several pictures from magazines and ask each group of children to sort the pictures according to ways in which they are the same. Invite a volunteer from each group to explain how the pictures were sorted and to explain that group's sorting rule.

Problem-Solving Applications: Take a Close Look

ACCESS CONTENT

Objective Review and apply key concepts, skills, and strategies learned in this chapter.

ESL Strategies

Use before CHECK ✓

🕙 10 MIN

> Use Total
Physical Response

Clear a space in the classroom for children to move around. Ask for three volunteers. **We are going to act out some of the words we have learned, such as** *middle, between, left,* **and** *right.* Ask one of the three children to stand in the middle, with his or her back to the class. **Pretend that your name is "Middle," okay? Can you raise your right hand, "Middle"?** Have a second child stand to the right of "Middle" (with his or her back to the class). Ask the class: **Is (Child B) standing to the right of "Middle" or the left of "Middle"?** Help children to recognize that the second child is standing to the right of "Middle." Name Child B "Right." **Can you raise your left hand, "Middle"?** Have the third child stand to the left of "Middle" (with his or her back to the class). **Is (Child C) standing to the right of "Middle" or the left of "Middle"?** Guide children to recognize that the third child is standing to the left of "Middle." Name Child C "Left."

Now ask another volunteer to direct you to stand next to "Middle," between "Left" and "Right." **Who is standing in the middle now? There are two of us in the middle now. There are two of us standing between "Left" and "Right."** Make room for another child to come and stand between you and "Middle." **Now how many of us are in the middle?** Help children count everyone standing in the middle. **Now there are three of us standing in the middle. Where are we standing? We are standing between "Left" and "Right."** Have the first group of children sit down and have a second group come up and repeat the exercise. If time allows, have a third group repeat as well.

As Many, More, and Fewer

ACCESS CONTENT

USE WITH LESSON
2-1

Objective Use one-to-one correspondence to compare two groups and determine whether one group has more, fewer, or as many as the other group.

Materials 4 chairs

Vocabulary As many (equal), more, fewer

ESL Strategies

Use Graphic ➤
Organizers

Use before LEARN

🕐 15–20 MIN

On the board, create a 2-column chart with "Girls" at the top of Column A and "Boys" at the top of Column B. Ask 3 girls and 3 boys for their names. Write the names in the appropriate columns. Draw lines connecting the adjacent girl and boy names. **Does each name have a "match-up," or are there some names left over?** *(Each name has a match-up, so there are no names left over.)* Guide children to count the names in each column aloud with you: **"1, 2, 3 girls. 1, 2, 3 boys." The number of girls and the number of boys are** equal**. There are** as many **girls as there are boys.** Ask 2 more girls for their names. Write their names in Column A. **Are there any girl's names left over now, any girl's names that don't have match-ups?** *(Yes, there are two girl's names that don't have match-ups.)* **That means that there are** more **girls than boys on our chart.** Guide children to count the names in each column with you: **"1, 2, 3, 4, 5 girls. 1, 2, 3 boys." So there are** fewer **boys than girls on our chart.** Continue the process, alternating among *as many, more,* and *fewer,* and connecting adjacent names with lines, as you compare Column A with Column B, until you have every child's name recorded on the chart. Ask children to draw a conclusion based on each comparison and to explain their decision each time.

Place a row of 4 chairs in front of the room. Ask 2 volunteers to sit in the chairs. Guide children to count with you: **"1, 2, 3, 4 chairs. 1, 2 children."** What do **we have more of?** *(Chairs)* Ask 2 more volunteers to sit in the remaining chairs. **What about now?** *(Now there are as many chairs as there are children.)* Have another volunteer come up. **Can (Child) sit down? Why not?** *(No, because there are more children than there are chairs.)* **How can we make it possible for (Child) to sit down?** *(Add another chair to the row of chairs at the front of the room.)* At each step, ask children to explain their reasoning.

Real Graphs

ACCESS CONTENT

USE WITH LESSON
2-2

Objective Make and read a real graph.

Materials Basket; 5 plates; 5 napkins; 5 spoons; 5 knives; 5 forks; masking tape

Vocabulary Graph, real graph

ESL Strategies   *Use before*   **LEARN** 10 MIN

Use Real Objects ➤

Tell children that you have invited 5 bears to come for tea. **But I want to make a <u>graph</u> to see whether or not we have enough supplies in our basket.** Hold up, in turn, 1 plate, 1 napkin, 1 spoon, 1 knife, and 1 fork. **How many of each of these things will we need for our guests?** Have children review how many bears are coming for tea. Explain that you can make a graph using the supplies in your basket. **When we use real objects to make a graph, it's called a <u>real graph</u>.** Show children each object and name it. Have volunteers come up and reach into your basket. Have them each take out one item, say its name, and help you tape it to the board, beginning at the bottom of the appropriate column and working upward. (See illustration.) Stop at some point, for example, when you have 2 knives and 3 spoons, among other objects, taped to the board. **Let's stop and look at our real graph so we can see what we have so far.**

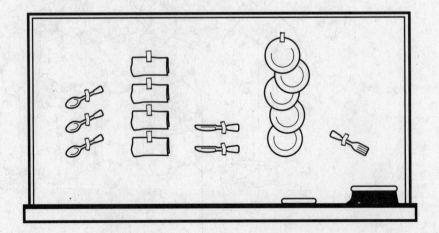

Have children count the number of items in each column. **Are there more spoons or knives?** *(Spoons)* Encourage children who are ready to produce complete sentences to say, "There are more spoons than knives." Continue to invite children to make more than/less than comparisons.

Expand Student ➤
Responses
Do we have enough knives for our 5 bear friends? *(No)* **Enough plates?** *(Yes)* **Napkins?** *(No)* **Forks?** *(No)* **Spoons?** *(No)* Count the items in each column again, and guide children to decide how many more of each object you will need in order to have enough for the 5 guests who are coming to tea. Have other volunteers take the additional items out of the basket and tape them to the graph. **Now let's check our real graph one last time.** Have the class count the items in each column aloud—and raise their hands when they think you have enough of a particular item for your tea with the 5 bears.

Picture Graphs

ACCESS CONTENT

USE WITH LESSON
2-3

Objective Make and read a picture graph.

Materials Unlined index cards, some with happy faces, some with suns; masking tape

Vocabulary Picture graph

ESL Strategies *Use before* **LEARN** 🕐 15–20 MIN

Use Graphic ➤
Organizers
We can use pictures to make a <u>picture graph</u>**. A picture graph can help us compare two groups. It can show us which group has more, and which group has fewer. Are you ready to make a picture graph?** Display the cards on which you have drawn (or stamped) happy faces and suns. *(Note:* You will need more cards than there are children so that there will be some remainders.) Shuffle the cards and place them facedown on a table. Have each child pick a card without letting the other children see it. **How many of you chose happy faces?** Have children who picked happy-face cards bring them to you. Tape the cards in a column on the board, beginning at the bottom of the board and moving up. (See illustration.) **How many of you chose suns?** Gather the sun cards and tape them in another column on the board. **Without counting the cards, how can you tell which group has more cards?** *(The group with more cards in it is taller.)* **Without counting, how can you tell which group has fewer?** *(The group with fewer cards in it is shorter.)* **Now let's count the cards to see if we are correct.** Count each group of cards with the children. **How many happy-face cards are there?** Record the number on the board. **How many sun cards are there?** Record the number on the board.

Use Small-Group ➤
Interactions
Have children work in small groups of three. Shuffle the cards. Ask each child to draw several cards from the pile. Then have children in each group work together to make their own picture graphs. Remind children to start the first column of cards at the bottom edge of the table or desk where they are working.

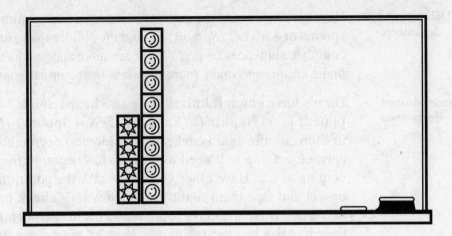

Bar Graphs

ACCESS CONTENT; EXTEND LANGUAGE

USE WITH LESSON
2-4

Objective Collect and organize data in a bar graph to answer a question.

Materials *(per group)* Blue and red construction-paper squares; masking tape; large sheet of white paper

Vocabulary Bar graph, survey

ESL Strategies | *Use before* **LEARN** | ⏲ 10 MIN

**Use
Demonstration** ➤ **Did you know that you can make a <u>bar graph</u> to find out the answer to a question? Let's do it!** At the top of the board write, "What Are You Wearing Today?"

Who's wearing pants today? Call on a few children. For each one wearing pants, tape a blue square onto the board to make a column. **Who's wearing a dress today?** Do the same with red squares, making another column. **Are more children wearing pants or dresses today? How can we tell?** *(Sample answer: The taller column of blue squares shows that more children are wearing pants.)* **How can we check to see whether or not we're right?** Guide children to count the number of squares in the first column aloud with you. Continue the process for the second column. Record both numbers on the board.

**Have Students
Report Back
Orally** ➤ Have children brainstorm questions that they want to ask of one another. Write three of those questions on the board. Then have children work in small groups. Give each group a stack of red and blue squares, some masking tape, and a large sheet of white paper. Tell children that they are to <u>survey</u> members in their group about one of the questions on the board and create their own bar graph. Then have one child from each group report to the class what his or her group found out and how group members represented the information on their bar graph.

Sound and Movement Patterns

ACCESS CONTENT

Objective Copy and extend sound and movement patterns.

Vocabulary Pattern, repeat

ESL Strategies

Use Total ➤
Physical Response

Use before CHECK ✓

🕐 10–15 MIN

Explain to children that you are going to show them how to play a game using <u>patterns</u>. Explain that a pattern is something that <u>repeats</u> over and over again. **Now listen very carefully to this pattern.** Demonstrate a simple sound pattern such as clap hands twice, tap desk twice; clap hands twice, tap desk twice; clap hands twice, tap desk twice. **What am I doing over and over again? What is my pattern?** Allow time for children to answer, either with words or by physically copying your pattern. **That's right. I'm clapping two times and then tapping two times. So my pattern is clap, clap, tap, tap—repeated over and over again: clap, clap, tap, tap; clap, clap, tap, tap; clap, clap, tap, tap.** Have children follow the pattern with you. Check to see that they are all following correctly. **Who can think of another kind of sound pattern?**

Now I am going to show you a different kind of pattern: a movement pattern. Watch me carefully. When you figure out my pattern, you can join in. Begin a simple movement pattern such as stand up, sit down, fold your arms; stand up, sit down, fold your arms; stand up, sit down, fold your arms. When all or most children have joined in, stop. **Can someone tell me what our movement pattern was?** *(Stand up, sit down, fold your arms.)* **Who can think of another kind of movement pattern?**

Color Patterns

ACCESS CONTENT

Objective Copy and extend color patterns.

Materials *(per pair)* 6 construction-paper triangles in 2 different colors (green, yellow, red, or blue); masking tape

ESL Strategies

Use ➤
Demonstration

Use before CHECK ✓

🕐 15–20 MIN

Hold up a green triangle. **What color is this triangle?** *(Green)* Tape the green triangle on the board. Hold up a yellow triangle. **What color is this triangle?** *(Yellow)* Tape the yellow triangle on the board, to the right of the green one. Continue the process, taping another green and another yellow triangle, and then another green and another yellow triangle, to the board. Point to each pair of shapes in turn and say their color names: **green, yellow; green, yellow; green, yellow. What color comes next?** *(Green)* **And after that?** *(Yellow)* Explain that this kind of pattern is called a color pattern. Guide children to understand and describe the pattern. Repeat the process again using red and blue triangles. Have children guess the pattern.

Use ➤
Peer Questioning

Organize children into pairs. Hand out 6 triangles in 2 different colors to each pair. Have one child make a color pattern on a table or desktop and then ask his or her partner, "What is my pattern?" Have the partner figure out the pattern, pointing to the first (core) element that is subsequently repeated in the pattern. Then have partners switch roles.

Shape Patterns

USE WITH LESSON 2-7

ACCESS CONTENT; EXTEND LANGUAGE

Objective Copy and extend shape patterns.

Materials Red construction-paper squares and triangles; masking tape; *(per child)* 3 same-colored sheets of construction paper (green, yellow, red, or blue); scissors; sheet of white paper; glue

ESL Strategies *Use before* **CHECK** ✓   🕐 15–20 MIN

Use ➤
Demonstration

Hold up a red square. **What shape is this?** *(A square)* Place the square on the chalk rail. Then hold up a red triangle. **What shape is this?** *(A triangle)* Place the triangle on the chalk rail to the right of the square. Repeat the pattern. Point to each shape in turn as you say its shape name: **square, triangle; square, triangle; square, triangle. Can anyone tell me what I am doing?** *(You are making a pattern.)* **That's right. If my pattern is square, triangle; square, triangle; square, triangle . . . what comes next?** *(Square)*

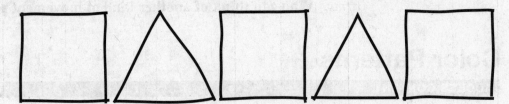

Have Students ➤
Report Back
Orally

This is called a shape pattern. Who can think of another kind of shape pattern? Create another pattern using a different combination of triangles and squares.

Hand out 3 sheets of same-colored construction paper to each child along with scissors, glue, and a sheet of white paper. Invite children to make shape patterns of their own choosing by (a) cutting the construction-paper rectangles into smaller shapes; (b) using those shapes to make a repeating shape pattern; (c) gluing their pattern onto white paper. Have volunteers display their patterns and explain them to the class. Exhibit patterns around the classroom.

Comparing Patterns

ACCESS CONTENT; EXTEND LANGUAGE

Objective Compare patterns to find how they are alike or different.

ESL Strategies ‖ *Use before* **LEARN** ⏲ 10 MIN

Use ➤
Demonstration

Review with children that a pattern is created by things such as sounds, colors, or shapes that repeat over and over again. Then invite two volunteers to the front of the class. Ask the first child to make a pattern using clapping and tapping. Have children join in until everyone understands the child's pattern. **What is (Child A's) pattern?** Make sure that all children understand the pattern. Then ask the second volunteer to create a different pattern using clapping and tapping. Invite children to join in the pattern. **What is (Child B's) pattern?** Again, make sure that all children understand the pattern.

Can we compare these two patterns? How are they the same? *(They both have clapping and tapping)* **How are they different?** *(Sample answer: The first pattern had two claps and then two taps repeated over and over; the second pattern had one clap and then one tap repeated over and over)*

Focus on Use ➤

Explain that the word *pattern* is used in many different ways. Prompt children to suggest some of these ways, such as music (as in a drumming pattern) and design (as in a tile pattern on the floor). **You can listen to a drummer play a pattern. You can look at a tile pattern on the floor. But can you compare these patterns? How are they different?** *(Sample answer: One is a sound pattern; the other is a shape pattern.)* **How are they alike?** *(Both have something that repeats: for example, one slow drumbeat followed by three fast drumbeats, over and over again; or black and white tiles that make a kind of zigzag pattern on the floor.)*

Problem-Solving Strategy: Look for a Pattern

ACCESS CONTENT; EXTEND LANGUAGE

Objective Solve problems by identifying patterns, determining the core that repeats, and showing the pattern in another way.

Materials Item with bold black-and-white stripes (such as a T-shirt); picture of a zebra; *(per child)* 2 crayons

ESL Strategies ‖ *Use before* **LEARN** ⏲ 10 MIN

Use Real Objects ➤ Show children an object such as a T-shirt that has bold black-and-white stripes. Explain that this is a pattern. Point to each stripe in turn as you

say: **black, white; black, white; black, white** (and so on). **Where does the pattern start to repeat?** *(It repeats after the first "black, white.")* Have children come up and point to the part that repeats.

Use Pictures ➤ Display the picture of a zebra. Have children discuss what kind of coat the zebra has. **It's a striped coat, and it's black and white.** Guide children to understand that the zebra has the same pattern as the T-shirt. **Where does the pattern on the zebra repeat?** *(It too repeats after the first "black, white.")* **So the pattern on the zebra is the same as the pattern on the T-shirt; it's just shown another way.**

Have Students Report Back Orally ➤ Give each child two different-colored crayons. Ask children to make their own patterns using the two colors. Then have them explain the pattern and point to where the pattern repeats.

Creating Patterns

USE WITH LESSON 2-10

ACCESS CONTENT

Objective Create and extend patterns.

Materials Dry macaroni in various colors and sizes; yarn

ESL Strategies | *Use before* **LEARN** 15–20 MIN

Use Demonstration ➤ Take several pieces of dry macaroni and make a necklace with an AB color pattern. Tie a knot on the end of a piece of yarn or string. Hold up the first piece of macaroni. **This is a piece of green macaroni. I am going to put it on this string. It will be the first part of my pattern.** Then hold up the next piece of macaroni. **This is a piece of red macaroni. I am going to put it on the string next to the green piece.** Review the pattern: **green, red.** Put another green and another red piece of macaroni on the string; then repeat the pattern again. Point to the six pieces: **green, red; green, red; green, red. What comes next?** *(Green)* **That's right. My pattern that repeats is green, red.** Ask if all children can see the pattern. If there are still children who are unsure of the pattern, review the pattern again.

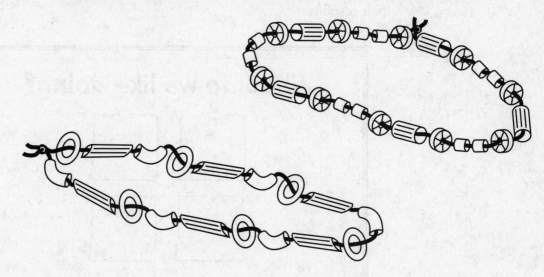

Use Manipulatives ➤ Invite the children to make their own necklaces out of macaroni. Hand out macaroni and yarn to the children. Provide at least three different kinds of macaroni that vary in size and/or color. Tell children to tie a knot on the end of their yarn and then to string one piece at a time. When children are done with their necklaces, have several volunteers explain the patterns they made.

Problem-Solving Applications: Favorite Things

USE WITH LESSON 2-11

ACTIVATE PRIOR KNOWLEDGE/BUILD BACKGROUND; ACCESS CONTENT

Objective Review and apply concepts, skills, and strategies learned in this and the previous chapter.

Materials Magazine pictures showing two popular activities such as reading or playing baseball

ESL Strategies | ***Use before*** **LEARN**

⏱ 10–15 MIN

Connect to Prior Experiences ➤ Have children discuss activities that they like to do at home. Write the activities on the board. Have children discuss when they like to do these activities and with whom. Write their responses on the board. Ask children to tell what activities they think are most popular with children in their class. If possible, ask them to explain why. You may also want to ask children about activities they liked to do in their native countries.

Use Graphic Organizers ➤ Tape pictures of 2 popular activities on the board, such as playing baseball and reading. Discuss the pictures. Then ask children to raise their hands if they prefer doing the activity in column 1 or the activity in column 2. Count the children's hands. In a vertical formation, draw an X for each raised hand. Afterwards, count the number of Xs in each column. Ask: **What do more children like doing?** Have children share their responses.

Counting 1, 2, and 3

USE WITH LESSON 3-1

ACCESS CONTENT

Objective Use objects to represent and count the quantities 1, 2, and 3.

Materials Number Cards 0–11 (Teaching Tool 12); sets of objects, such as 1 book, 2 markers, 3 crayons; *(per child)* 3 sheets of paper; markers

Vocabulary One, two, three, count

ESL Strategies   *Use before* **LEARN** 15–20 MIN

Use Demonstration ➤ Display the number cards for 1, 2, and 3. Next to each card, display a corresponding set of objects, such as 1 book, 2 markers, and 3 crayons. Hold up the book. **How many books do I have?** *(1)* Hold up the 2 markers. **Now let's count how many markers I have.** Guide children to count the markers aloud with you: **"One, two." I have 2 markers in all.** Hold up the 3 crayons. **And how many crayons do I have?** As you point to each crayon in turn, have children count aloud with you: **"One, two, three." I have 3 crayons in all.**

Use Peer Questioning ➤ Divide the class into pairs. Give each child 3 sheets of paper. Tell children to draw a picture that shows one, such as one apple or one banana. Then have them draw a picture that shows two of something. Finally, have them draw a picture that shows three of something. One child in each pair can ask the other: "Can you show me one?" The other child in that pair should then show his or her partner the picture that shows one thing and say the number aloud. Partners repeat for two and three. Then they exchange roles.

Reading and Writing 1, 2, and 3

USE WITH LESSON 3-2

ACCESS CONTENT

Objective Recognize and write the numerals that describe the quantities 1, 2, and 3.

Materials *(per child)* 1 sheet of paper with a large number 1, 2, or 3 written on it: "1" in green, "2" in red, "3" in blue; a green, red, or blue marker: green for "1"; red for "2"; blue for "3"

Vocabulary Number

ESL Strategies   *Use before* **LEARN** 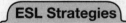 10–15 MIN

Use Gestures ➤ Pass out the sheets of paper marked with large numerals. **Some of you have the number 1 on your papers; some of you have the number 2; and some of you have the number 3. Who has the number 1?** Show children how to use their index fingers to trace the number 1 as they say the word aloud. **Who has the number 2? Who has the number 3?** Have children continue to use gestures to trace each number as they say it aloud.

What color is the number 1? *(Green)* **The number 2?** *(Red)* **The number 3?** *(Blue)* Have all of the "number 1" children hold up their papers. Explain that you want each of them to draw 1 green circle to match the number 1 on their papers. Demonstrate on the board. Have all of the "number 2" children hold up their papers. **How many circles do you think these children should draw on their papers?** *(2 circles)* **And what color should those circles be?** *(Red)* Have all of the "number 3" children hold up their papers. **How many circles do you think these children should draw on their papers?** *(3 circles)* **And what color should those circles be?** *(Blue)* **Okay, who needs a green marker? A red marker? A blue marker?** Pass out the colored markers as children raise their hands. Ask children to draw the correct color and number of circles on their papers. Ask for volunteers to hold up their papers. **Let's check this paper. I see the number 2 printed in red. And I see 2 circles drawn in red.** Have children in each "number group" count their circles aloud with you. Invite more volunteers to show their papers and invite the class to check the color and count the circles aloud with you.

Counting 4 and 5

ACCESS CONTENT; ACTIVATE PRIOR KNOWLEDGE/BUILD BACKGROUND

USE WITH LESSON
3-3

Objective Use objects to represent and count the quantities 4 and 5.

Materials Picture of a grocery store; items for a "grocery store," such as 4 cans of soup, 4 potatoes, 4 apples, 5 oranges, 5 bagels

Vocabulary Four, five

ESL Strategies | *Use before* **LEARN** | ⏱ 10–15 MIN

Use Real Objects ➤ Write the numbers 4 and 5 on the board. Create a line of 4 oranges on the chalk tray. **We can count to four using these oranges.** Invite children to count aloud with you as you count the group of four oranges. Place another orange in the row. **Now let's count to five, using these oranges.** Have children count aloud with you as you point to each orange in turn: **"One, two, three, four, five."** Roll the fifth orange back and forth (away from the group and then back to the group) as you ask the class to tell you how many oranges there are in the group. **Now there are 4. And now there are 5**.

Connect to Prior Experiences ➤ Show a picture of a grocery store. **Who has gone to a grocery store?** Talk about what happens when people shop: they buy items in certain amounts, for example, 1 box of cereal, 2 tomatoes, 3 bottles of water, and so on.

Set up a "grocery store" on a table where everything in the store comes in quantities of four or five. Set up each group separately, that is, somewhat removed from the other groups.

Use Role Playing ➤ Invite one volunteer to play the grocery store clerk, another to play the shopper. Have the shopper ask for four apples. Guide the clerk through counting out the right amount. Have the class count aloud with you and the clerk: **"1, 2, 3, 4 apples."** Have another pair of children volunteer, with the shopper asking for five cans of soup. Have the class count aloud with the clerk as he or she counts out 5 cans of soup. Have other pairs of volunteers come forward. Each time, invite the class to count the correct number of items aloud. Finally, ask the class how many different kinds of items are in your grocery store. Have volunteers hold up 1 can of soup, 1 potato, 1 apple, 1 orange, and 1 bagel. **If I want to buy one of everything, how many things would I be buying in all?** *(5 things)* Guide the class to understand that 1 each of 5 different kinds of items adds up to a total of 5 items in all.

Reading and Writing 4 and 5

USE WITH LESSON
3-4

ACCESS CONTENT

Objective Recognize and write the numerals that describe the quantities 4 and 5.

Materials *(per child)* 1 sheet of paper with a large 4 or 5 written on it; finger paints; 2 large sheets of paper

ESL Strategies

Use before **CHECK** ✓

⏱ 10 MIN

Use Gestures ➤ Distribute the papers with 4 or 5 written on them. Remind children that when they learned to read and write the numbers 1, 2, and 3, they traced the shapes with their fingers. **Now we can do that with the number 4 and the number 5.** Have children use their index fingers to trace each number as they say it aloud. Invite children to describe the design of each numeral. *(Sample answer: 4 has a short straight line, a sideways line, and then a long straight line.)* **Can you trace the number 4 in the air? Try it. Can you trace the number 5 in the air? Try it.** Then ask the class to instruct you (using words and/or gestures) as you print each of the numerals on the board. Guide children through giving you the right directions or showing you the right gestures until they've told you how to write a legible 4 and 5.

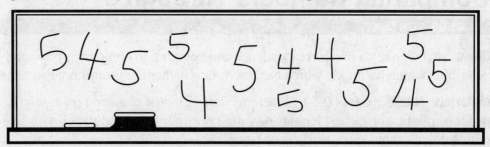

Use Total Physical Response ➤ To provide each child with more opportunities to explore the numbers 4 and 5, distribute fingerpaints and two large sheets of paper. Tell children to put finger paints on their fingers and to use their fingers to write lots of 4s on one paper and lots of 5s on the other paper.

Reading and Writing 0

USE WITH LESSON
3-5

ACCESS CONTENT

Objective Recognize and write the numeral that describes the quantity 0.

Materials 7 pencils; *(per group)* Number Cards 0–11 (Teaching Tool 12); pencils; plastic container; box; 5 balls

Vocabulary Zero

ESL Strategies *Use before* LEARN ⏱ 10–15 MIN

Paraphrase Ideas ➤ Give a child 5 pencils. **(Child A) has 5 pencils. Look what happens when I take them away.** Take all 5 of the pencils away from the child. **Now (Child A) has no pencils. (Child A) has zero pencils.** Give another child 2 pencils. **How many pencils does (Child B) have?** *(2)* Take the pencils away. **Now how many pencils does (Child B) have?** *(None, zero)* **That's right, (Child B) has zero pencils.** Write the number 0 on the board.

Use Real Objects ➤ Display the number cards for 0–5 along with a group of pencils. Hold up the number 3 card. **What card am I holding up? How many pencils should I hold up?** Invite children to count the pencils aloud with you. Continue this process with other numbers before picking the zero card. **Now how many pencils should I hold up?** Encourage children to tell you to hold up zero pencils. **Why shouldn't I hold up any pencils?** *(Because zero means none)*

Use Small-Group Interactions ➤ Have children work in small groups. Give each group a set of number cards for 0–5, a box, a plastic container, and 5 balls. Have children place the number cards in the container. Have one volunteer draw a number card. **What number do you have?** *(2)* **How many balls will you put into the box?** *(2)* Have the child put 2 balls into the box as he or she counts the balls aloud: "1, 2." Have the child take the balls back out of the box. **What if the card you draw is the 0 card? How many balls would you put in the box?** *(None; zero)* Have children proceed, taking turns drawing number cards and placing the correct number of balls in the box each time.

Comparing Numbers Through 5

USE WITH LESSON
3-6

ACCESS CONTENT

Objective Use one-to-one correspondence and counting to compare groups and determine which has more, which has fewer, or whether the groups are the same.

Materials Number Cards 0–11 (Teaching Tool 12), pipe cleaners; *(per pair)* 2 paper or plastic cups; short lengths of yarn; construction paper; paper with line drawn down center; glue, markers or pencils

Vocabulary More, less, fewer, same (equal)

Use ➤
Demonstration

Display a group of 2 pipe cleaners and 5 pipe cleaners, respectively. Have a child count the pipe cleaners in each group and say the number aloud. Put number cards next to the two sets. Then ask: **Which group has more pipe cleaners?** *(The group with 5 pipe cleaners)* Continue in this manner using numbers from 1–5 until all children have had a turn. Then continue the activity by asking: **Which group has fewer, or less, pipe cleaners?** Finally display two equal groups. **These groups are the same. They contain the same number of pipe cleaners. Let's count them.** Explain that when two groups have the same number of items, they are equal.

Use Real Objects ➤

Give pairs of children two cups with 1–5 small objects such as yarn, noodles or paper clips in each cup. Have children empty the contents of each cup onto a separate sheet of construction paper. Have them count the objects in one group and write the number on the paper. Then have them repeat for the other group. Ask them to identify whether one group has more, fewer or the same amount of objects. Give them a piece of paper with a line drawn down the middle. Have them glue one group of objects on each side of the paper. Ask each child to write one of the numbers. Ask one child to circle the number of the group that has more. Have the other child draw a line under the number of the group that has fewer or less. If the groups have the same number, have them draw a box around each number.

Ordering Numbers 0 Through 5

ACCESS CONTENT

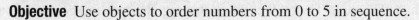

USE WITH LESSON
3-7

Objective Use objects to order numbers from 0 to 5 in sequence.

Materials Number Cards 0–11 (Teaching Tool 12); set of 6 index cards, each marked with from 0 to 5 large dots

Vocabulary Order

ESL Strategies *Use before* **CHECK** 🕐 10–15 MIN

Use ➤
Demonstration

Display the number cards 0–5 in order. **Are these cards are in order?** Point to each card in turn as you say the number on it. Have children say the number with you. **The cards are in order because they begin at 0 and go up to 5.** Make sure the class understands the order of the number cards.

Display the 1-dot card. **How many dots are on this card?** *(1)* Have children count the dot aloud with you: **"1 dot."** Point to the number 1 card. **What number is this?** *(1)* Place the 1-dot card beneath the number 1 card. **The dot card matches the number card.** Repeat with the 2-dot card. **We can order the dot cards by counting the number of dots on the cards. After we count the dots, we can match the dot card to the correct number card.** Invite children to help you match the next dot card to its corresponding number card: **"1, 2, 3 dots." What number card does this dot card go**

with? Yes, the number 3 card. Proceed to line up all of the dot cards with their corresponding number cards. Then have children check the order with you by counting the dots on each dot card aloud. **What did we do? We put the dot cards in order.** Finally, point out that each number, beginning with the number 1, has one more dot on its dot card than the number before it has on its dot card.

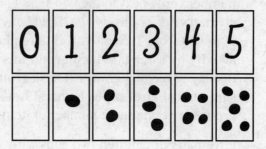

Problem-Solving Strategy: Make a Graph

USE WITH LESSON 3-8

ACCESS CONTENT

Objective Solve problems by making and reading a real graph and a picture graph.

Materials Basket containing 5 pencils, 4 crayons, 2 paint brushes, 1 marker; masking tape

Vocabulary Most, fewest

ESL Strategies

Use before **LEARN**

⏲ 10–15 MIN

Use Real Objects ➤ Tell children that you have a basket full of items to paint and color with. Take out each item and name it. Then tell children that together you are going to use the items to make a real graph. Explain that this graph, made of real things, will help them understand the ideas of <u>most</u> and <u>fewest</u>. **Let's make this graph now.** Have a volunteer reach into your basket and take out one item (a crayon, pencil, paint brush, marker). Tape it to the board. Have volunteers take more items out of the bag that you tape to the board. Be sure to line the items up carefully in columns, with each item taking up the same amount of vertical space. Continue until you have taped all the items onto the graph. Explain that the tallest column has the most items in it. The shortest column has the fewest.

Use Graphic Organizers ➤ Tell children that this same information can also be shown in a different kind of graph such as a picture graph. Explain that a picture graph uses pictures to present information. Point to the real graph and say: **How many pencils are there?** (5) **That's right. So I will draw 5 pencils in this first column.** Below the column write the word "pencils" and read it aloud. **Now, I will look at this next column. How many crayons are there?** (4) **That's right, so I will draw 4 crayons in my picture graph.** Then write the word "crayons" beneath the column and read it aloud. Continue in this manner until the picture graph is completed. Then ask children to describe the similarities between both graphs. You may want to explain that the number of items in the graphs remain the same whether it is shown in a real graph or a picture graph.

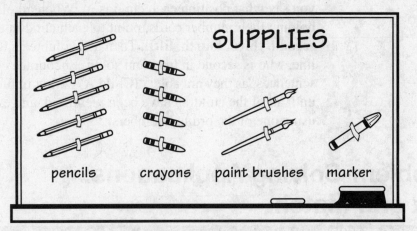

Ordinal Numbers Through Fifth

ACCESS CONTENT; EXTEND LANGUAGE

Objective Use the words first through fifth to identify ordinal positions.

Materials Number Cards 0–11 (Teaching Tool 12)

Vocabulary First, second, third, fourth, fifth

ESL Strategies

Use before CHECK ✓   ⏱ 10–15 MIN

Use Demonstration ➢ Count slowly from 1 to 5 with children. Then display the number cards for 1–5 in random order. Have the class count again from 1 to 5. This time, while children are counting, have a volunteer put the cards in correct order in the chalk tray. **Now let's look at the cards and say the numbers.** Point to each card in turn as you say: **Number 1 is the first number. Number 2 is the second number. Number 3 is the third number. Number 4 is the fourth number. Number 5 is the fifth number.** Point to the cards again and say: **First, second, third fourth, fifth.** Have children repeat the ordinals aloud with you.

Invite five children to stand in line. Give the first child the number card for 1. **You are first in line.** Give the second child the number card for 2. **You are second in line.** Continue with three more children, inviting the class to help you say what position each child is in. When all of the children are in line holding their number cards, point to each child in turn and say: **First, second, third, fourth, fifth.** Then ask volunteers to identify who is first in line, who is second in line, and so on. Encourage children to use complete sentences, as they are able: "(Child A) is first in line." Continue this process until all of the children have been identified, and everyone has had a turn using one of the ordinal numbers.

Problem-Solving Applications: Mix and Match

USE WITH LESSON 3-10

`ACCESS CONTENT`

Objective Review and apply concepts, skills, and strategies learned in this and previous chapters.

Materials 2 red and 3 blue construction paper squares; tape; (*per pair*) cut-out shapes from construction paper; glue

ESL Strategies | ***Use before*** `LEARN` | 🕐 15–20 MIN

Use Demonstration ➤ Display 2 red and 3 blue squares. Place each shape on the board randomly and name it. With a piece of chalk, draw a line connecting the 2 red squares. Say: **These match. They are both red. Are there any other red shapes?** (*No*) **Let's write the number of red squares here.** Write 2 somewhere beneath the shapes. Then tell children that you will match the blue squares. Draw a line connecting 2 of the blue squares. Have children notice that 1 square is left over. Say: **There is one shape left over. What is it?** (*A blue square*) **Now I will write the number of blue squares here. Let's count them together.** Write the number 3 below the blue squares. Then circle the number 3. Say: **3 is greater than 2. That means there are more blue squares than red squares.** Repeat the process again with a different number of shapes.

Use Small-Group Interactions ➤ Provide pairs with a small number of cut out shapes in two colors. Have them glue the shapes onto construction paper. In a one-to-one fashion, have them connect the shapes that are the same color and write the total number on the paper. Have them repeat the process for the shapes of the other color. Then have them circle the number that is more, and underline the number that is less. As you visit each pair, have them describe their process.

Counting 6 and 7

ACCESS CONTENT

USE WITH LESSON
4-1

Objective Use objects to represent and count the quantities 6 and 7.

Materials *(per pair)* Index cards with a large 6 or 7 written on each one; cup of small items, such as buttons or pennies

Vocabulary Six, seven, one more

ESL Strategies   *Use before* **LEARN**   10 MIN

Use Real Objects ➤ Show children the index cards. **Here's a** <u>six</u>. **Here's a** <u>seven</u>. **What can you tell me about the numbers six and seven?** Have children count aloud to six, and then to seven. **6 is** <u>one more</u> **than 5. And 7 is one more than 6.** Tell children that they will make groups of objects showing the numbers 6 and 7. Explain that they can play a game using the cards and the buttons (or whatever small items you have gathered together).

Ask a volunteer to come up and play a sample game with you. **Here's our cup of buttons. And here are our number cards.** Ask the child to pick a card and hold it up for you and the class to see. **(Child A) picked the number 6. So I will use some of our buttons to show the number 6.** Count from 1 up to 6 as you take each of 6 buttons out of your cup and place it on the table in front of you. **Why did I lay down 6 buttons?** *(To go with the 6 card; to show the number 6)* **I laid down 6 buttons because (Child) picked the number 6.** Put the buttons back in the cup. **Now let's switch. This time, I will pick a 7 card. And (Child) will count out and lay down 7 buttons.** Have the class count the buttons aloud as you and your partner point to each one in turn. **(Child) laid down 7 buttons because I picked the 7 card. Which is more, 6 buttons or 7 buttons?** *(7 buttons)* **How many more?** *(One more)*

Use Small-Group Interactions ➤ Have children work in pairs. Pass out the cards and cups of buttons. Guide children through the process. **Which card did you pick?** Have that partner say the number. **How many buttons should your partner pick?** Have the other child count out the buttons. **Your partner can say, "I picked 6 buttons because he picked the 6 card."** Have partners take turns. As they play, have them discuss each other's cards and buttons using complete sentences, as they are able.

Counting 8

ACCESS CONTENT; EXTEND LANGUAGE

Objective Use objects to represent and count the quantity 8.

Materials *(per group)* Counters; *(per child)* 1 sheet of paper

Vocabulary Eight, one fewer

ESL Strategies *Use before* **LEARN** ⏱ 10–15 MIN

Use Demonstration ➤ Display one counter and ask children to count aloud with you: **"One."** Lay out another counter and ask children to continue counting: "Two." Repeat until you reach the seventh counter. **If I add one more counter, how many counters will I have in all?** *(8)* **Yes, I will have** <u>eight</u> **counters in all.** Place an eighth counter along with the others. Then have children count to eight with you as you point to each counter in turn: **"1, 2, 3, 4, 5, 6, 7, 8." If I take away one counter, how many counters will I have in all?** *(7)* Take one counter away and have a volunteer count the number of remaining counters aloud. **Are 7 counters** <u>one fewer</u> **or one more than 8 counters?** *(One fewer)* Take away another counter. **What is one fewer than 7?** *(6)* Continue doing this until no counters are left. Then encourage children to count aloud independently, as you again lay out the eight counters one at a time.

Have Students Report Back Orally ➤ Divide the class into groups. Then distribute counters to each group. Have group members work together to count out 8 counters. Invite them to figure out how many groups of 8 they have in all. Ask each child to draw circles to show his or her group's sets of 8 on a sheet of paper. Then discuss as a class what children have found. **Which group has the most groups of 8? Which group has the fewest groups of 8?**

Reading and Writing 6, 7, and 8

ACCESS CONTENT

Objective Recognize and write the numerals that describe the quantities 6, 7, and 8.

Materials *(per child)* 3 pipe cleaners; 3 sheets of paper with a large 6, 7, or 8 written on each one; clay; *(per pair)* dishpan filled with sand or cornmeal

Vocabulary Forward

ESL Strategies *Use before* **LEARN** ⏱ 15–20 MIN

Use Total Physical Response ➤ Tell children that they will learn more about reading and writing the numbers 6, 7, and 8. **You've already learned how to count** <u>forward</u> **from 0 to 5. Now listen as I count forward from 6 to 8: 6, 7, 8.** You may want to write each number on the board and point to it as you say it aloud. Invite children to count along with you.

Give each child a pipe cleaner and a piece of paper on which the number 6 is written. **This is the number 6. Let's say it aloud.** Demonstrate how to shape the number 6 out of a pipe cleaner. Have children bend the pipe cleaner into a 6 using the number written on the paper as a guide. Have children place the pipe cleaner over, or next to, the 6 on the paper to check their work. Next, give each child some clay. Tell children to make a snake shape out of the clay. Have them use their pipe-cleaner numbers and written numerals to help them shape their clay numbers.

Repeat this activity for the numbers 7 and 8.

Use Gestures ➤ **Now we are going to practice writing our numbers.** Divide the class into pairs and give each pair a container, such as a dishpan, filled with cornmeal or sand. First, have children trace each pipe-cleaner number with their index fingers. Then have them each use the same finger to write the number in the cornmeal or in the sand.

One child can then hold the pipe-cleaner number to his or her partner's back, and trace it with his or her finger. The other child can guess what number is being traced.

Counting 9 and 10

USE WITH LESSON
4-4

ACCESS CONTENT

Objective Use objects to count and represent the quantities 9 and 10.

Materials Ten-Frame (Workmat 4); Number Cards 0–11 (Teaching Tool 12); two-color counters

Vocabulary Nine, ten, backward

ESL Strategies *Use before* **LEARN** 🕐 10–15 MIN

Use Manipulatives ➤ Give each child 10 counters and a set of number cards 1–10. Say: **One.** Have children show the correct number card. Then have them show the same number of counters. Continue in this manner until all children have had an opportunity to form the correct number of counters to match the numbers on the number cards. When you get to <u>ten</u>, you may want to point out that 10 is made up of 2 numbers—1 and 0.

Then tell children: **We just counted forward from 1 to 10. Now let's count backward from 10 to 1.** Using their ten-frames, have children form the correct group of counters to match each number card. Say: **Ten.** Have children place 10 counters on their ten-frames. To show <u>nine</u>, tell children that they need to remove 1 counter. Continue in this manner to 1.

Use Small-Group ➤ Give each pair number cards from 8–10, 10 counters, and a ten-frame. Have
Interactions one child, pick a number card and read its number aloud. Then have the other child put the appropriate number of counters on the ten-frame. Encourage them to repeat this process several times, counting both forward and backward.

Reading and Writing 9 and 10

ACCESS CONTENT

Objective Recognize and write the numerals that describe the quantities 9 and 10.

Materials *(per child)* 10 pennies; paper and pencil

ESL Strategies   *Use before*   **LEARN**   ⏱ 10–15 MIN

Use ➤ **Here are 9 pennies. Let's count them together.** Point to each penny in
Demonstration turn as you count the members of the set in unison. Write the number 9 on the board. Read the number aloud as you point to it. Add another penny to the set of 9. **Now how many pennies do I have?** *(10)* **I have 10 pennies. Let's count them together.** Again, point to each penny in turn as you count in unison.

Explain that you are going to make a drawing showing the number 9. Demonstrate by placing the 9 pennies close together, but not touching one another, on a table. Place a piece of paper over them and rub the pencil lightly over each penny until an etching of the shape appears. Repeat this process for each penny. When completed, hold up your drawing so that all children can see it. Write the number 9 clearly in a lower corner of the paper. Reinforce the concept of 9 by counting each penny shape etched on the paper together as a class.

Repeat the process for the number 10.

Use Real Objects ➤ Have children make their own etchings of the pennies in groups of 9 and/or 10.

Comparing Numbers Through 10

ACCESS CONTENT

Objective Compare two numbers using sets of objects and one-to-one correspondence to determine which number is greater and which is less.

Materials Crayons; books; bottle tops; 5 sheets of construction paper to be used as picture cards (see below)

Vocabulary Greater, less

Use Real Objects ➤ Display groups of 3 and 9 crayons. Count the objects in each group with children. Ask for a volunteer to come forward. **Which group has more crayons in it?** *(The group with 9)* Explain that the number 9 is <u>greater</u> than the number 3. **What are some other numbers that are greater than the number 3?** *(4, 5, 6, …)* Display a group of 6 books and a group of 2 books. Count the books in each group with children. Then ask for a volunteer to identify the group that has more. *(The group with 6)* **This means that 6 is greater than 2.** Make sure that children understand the concept of greater. If children are having difficulty, review the concept again. Continue with groups of bottle tops. Then repeat the activity, having children find the group with fewer bottle tops in it. **4 bottle caps are fewer than 6 bottle caps; 4 is <u>less</u> than 6. 6 is greater than 4, and 4 is less than 6.** Encourage children to use the terms *greater than* and *less than* as they work.

Use Total Physical Response ➤ Display 2 books in one pile and a pile of more books next to it. Ask a child to come forward and count the 2 books aloud. **Can you make a group with more than 2 books in it? With fewer than 2 books in it?** Continue in this manner, having children make groups and compare numbers to determine which number is greater, and which number is less.

Give Frequent Feedback ➤ Make 5 picture cards that show groups of objects ranging from 1 to 10. (See illustration.) Ask for 4 volunteers and give one card to each. Save the card showing a group of 6 for yourself. Call one volunteer forward and tell the child to hold up his or her card. Count the objects on the card aloud with the class. **Look at my card and count the number of objects on it.** Count with children. **Does (Child) have more objects or fewer objects than I have? So which number is more, (Child's) number or my number? Which number is less?** Repeat with other volunteers and other number comparisons.

Does Robert's card have a greater number of things on it than my card has?

Comparing Numbers to 5 and 10

USE WITH LESSON
4-7

EXTEND LANGUAGE; ACCESS CONTENT

Objective Given a number from 1 through 10, tell whether it is more or less than 5 and whether it is less than 10.

Materials *(per pair)* 3 index cards

Vocabulary More than, fewer than

Focus on Meaning ➤ Hold up 2 fingers on one hand. **How many fingers do you see?** Count the 2 fingers aloud as you point to each one. Make sure that everyone agrees that you are holding up 2 fingers on one hand. Hold up 4 fingers on your other hand. Count the 4 fingers aloud as you point to each one. **Which hand has more fingers "standing up"?** *(The hand with 4 fingers)* **How do you know?** *(Because one hand has only 2 fingers "standing up" and the other has 4 fingers "standing up")* **Look at these 2 fingers. Look at these 4 fingers. The number 4 is** <u>more than</u> **the number 2. Can you tell me some other numbers that are more than the number 2?** *(3, 4, 5, ...)*

What other word do you know that means the same as more than? *(Greater)* Explain that *greater* and *more than* mean almost the same thing and that the term *more than* is often used to describe many things. Ask children to think of times when they, or someone else, has had more of something. **Did anyone ever have more pennies than you had? How did you know that that person had more than you had?** Repeat the process for <u>*fewer than*</u>. Explain that *fewer* and *less* are two words that mean almost the same thing. For instance, your class may have fewer children in it than the class next door has. **Our class has 23 children in it, and the class next door has 25 children. 23 children is fewer than 25 children. And 23 is less than 25.**

Give Frequent ➤ Have children work in pairs, sitting across from each other. Hand each pair 3
Feedback index cards. Tell one child in each pair to write down a number on each card between 1 and 10, but not including 5 or 10. Write the numbers 1 through 10 in horizontal sequence on the board and then cross out the 5 and the 10 to help children understand what you are saying. Also, tell them to keep their partners from seeing what they are writing. Have the child who does the writing place one of the cards facedown on the table, so that the other child cannot see it. Invite the second child to try to guess the number by asking questions. "Is the number more than 5 or less than 5?" If Child A says that the number is less than 5, then Child B tries to guess the number until he or she guesses correctly. You may need to explain that if the answer is more than 5, then the answer will have to be between 6 and 9. Some children may be able to ask and answer questions such as "Is the number closer to 6 or 10?" (especially if they refer to the numbers you have written on the board). Continue playing until all of the cards have been used and both children have had an opportunity to guess all of the numbers correctly.

Ordering Numbers 0 Through 10

ACCESS CONTENT

Objective Use a number line to order numbers from 0 through 10.

Materials Butcher paper; counters or beans; *(per child)* 1 large index card numbered with a number from 1 to 10

Vocabulary Before, after

ESL Strategies **Use before** LEARN

Use Manipulatives ➤ Draw a long number line on a piece of butcher paper large enough so that all children can see it clearly. Then write the numbers 1–10, spaced rather widely apart, below the line. Place objects, such as counters or beans, above the line to represent each number: one counter above 1; two counters above 2; and so on. Then model counting on the number line for children. As you say each number aloud, point to the corresponding numeral on the number line. **Let's count together: "1, 2, 3, 4, 5, 6, 7, 8, 9, 10."** Repeat several times. Then encourage children to count aloud independently as they take turns pointing to the numbers on the number line.

After children show that they are comfortable with counting to 10, return to the number line and count aloud, but this time stop after 5. **What number comes <u>after</u> 5?** Explain that the number 6 comes after the number 5. Continue counting to 8. **What number comes after number 8?** *(9)* Count to 3. **What number comes <u>before</u> number 3?** *(2)* Repeat this procedure with several numbers, modeling and discussing the concepts of before and after each time. When you refer to numbers by their ordinal names, overemphasize the pronunciation of the "th" as you say the words *fourth* and *fifth.* Many English language learners have trouble hearing the difference between *four* and *fourth, six* and *sixth,* and so on.

Use Pantomime ➤ Hand out one large-sized, numbered index card facedown to each of 10 children. Tell children to turn the cards over and to read the numbers on their cards. Then have the children form a line, starting, at left, with the child who holds the "1" card and ending, at right, with the child who holds the "10" card. Invite the rest of the children to count aloud as you walk behind the line and tap the appropriate child on the top of his or her head.

Have the 10 children trade places with someone in line so that all of the numbers are out of sequence. Then call on volunteers to help reorder the line by giving one direction at a time: "Alvin, go back to the front of the line." "Shannon, go stand next to Alvin." And so on.

Ordinal Numbers Through Tenth

USE WITH LESSON
4-9

ACCESS CONTENT

Objective Use the words *sixth* through *tenth* to identify ordinal positions.

Materials Number Cards 0–11 (Teaching Tool 12)

Vocabulary Sixth, seventh, eighth, ninth, tenth

ESL Strategies **Use before** LEARN

 10–15 MIN

Use Demonstration ➤ Count slowly from 1 to 10 with children. Display the number cards for 1–10 in random order. Have the class count again from 1 to 10, but this time, while everyone is counting, have a couple of volunteers help you position the cards in correct order in the chalk tray. **Now let's look at the cards and say the**

numbers. Point to each card in turn as you say: **Number 1 is the first number. Number 2 is the second number. Number 3 is the third number. Number 4 is the fourth number. Number 5 is the fifth number.** Continue in this manner for the ordinal numbers <u>sixth</u>, <u>seventh</u>, <u>eighth</u>, <u>ninth</u>, and <u>tenth</u>. Then point to the cards again, saying: **First, second, third fourth, fifth, sixth, seventh, eighth, ninth, and tenth.**

Use Total ➤
Physical Response

Invite 10 children to stand in a line—one in front of the other, facing right. Give the first child (the one at the far-right end of the line) the number card for 1. **You are first in line.** Give the second child the number card for 2. **You are second in line.** Continue in this manner with the remaining children. When all of the children are holding a card, point to each child in turn as you say: **First, second, third, fourth, fifth, sixth, seventh, eighth, ninth, tenth.** Ask a child to identify who is sixth in line. Encourage him or her to use a full sentence with the ordinal number: "(Child) is sixth in line." Then ask another child to identify who is seventh in line. Continue this process for the eighth, ninth, and tenth positions.

Problem-Solving Strategy:
Look for a Pattern

EXTEND LANGUAGE; ACCESS CONTENT

USE WITH LESSON
4-10

Objective Solve problems by copying and extending growing patterns.

Materials *(per pair)* 10 color tiles; 2-Centimeter Grid (Teaching Tool 46)

Vocabulary Growing pattern

ESL Strategies | *Use before* **LEARN** | 5–10 MIN

Focus on Meaning ➤ Explain to children that they are going to learn about a kind of pattern called a <u>growing pattern</u>. Say **growing pattern** slowly. **What does the word** *grow* **mean?** *(Children may offer responses such as "get bigger.")* **Who can use the word** *grow* **in a sentence?** *(Sample response: We will grow tomatoes in our garden.)* **Who can use the word** *growing* **in a sentence?** *(Sample response: The puppy is growing larger.)*

When children seem to feel comfortable with the word *growing,* ask: **What is a pattern?** *(Children may explain that a pattern is something that happens over and over again.)* If not, feel free to pantomime or illustrate a simple growing pattern, using hand claps: 1 clap; 2 claps; 3 claps. **What did I do to make my pattern grow?** *(Added one more clap each time)* **Who can tell me what I would need to do to keep growing this pattern?** *(Keep adding one more clap each time.)* Begin again with 1 clap and work your way up to 6 claps.

Use Total ➤
Physical Response

Divide the class into pairs and distribute 10 color tiles and a copy of Teaching Tool 46 to each pair. Show children how to begin a simple growing pattern, perhaps by placing 1 color tile in the first row of the grid, 2 color tiles in the second row, and so on. Encourage children to create their own growing patterns and describe them to the class.

Problem-Solving Applications: Let's Have a Picnic

ACCESS CONTENT; ACTIVATE PRIOR KNOWLEDGE/BUILD BACKGROUND

Objective Review and apply concepts, skills, and strategies learned in this and previous chapters.

Materials 3 blocks; *(per group)* 3–6 blocks

ESL Strategies   *Use before* **LEARN**   10–15 MIN

Use Pantomime ➤

Invite 4 volunteers to be rabbits. Invite children to brainstorm what they know about rabbits. Then ask children to name the foods they know rabbits eat, such as carrots, lettuce, strawberries, etc.

Clear an area for the "rabbits" and tell them that this is the farmer's garden. Display 3 blocks and tell them that these are carrots. Have the children pantomime being rabbits. Then ask them to each take a "carrot." Have children notice that there are not enough carrots for each rabbit. **How many carrots are there?** *(3)* **How many rabbits are there?** *(4)* **That's right. There are 4 rabbits but only 3 carrots. How many rabbits do not have carrots?** *(1)* **What could you do so that every rabbit has a carrot?** *(Give 1 carrot to the rabbit.)* Then repeat the activity with 5 carrots and explain that there are more carrots than rabbits.

Use Role Playing ➤

Divide children into small groups of four. Provide groups with 3–6 "carrots." Have them role-play being rabbits. Then have them determine whether they have more or less carrots than rabbits. Have volunteers explain how many rabbits are in their group, the number of carrots, and whether there are enough for each rabbit.

Counting 11 to 20

USE WITH LESSON
5-1

EXTEND LANGUAGE; ACCESS CONTENT

Objective Use objects to represent and count the quantities 11 through 20.

Materials *(per child)* Ten-Frame (Workmat 4); Double Ten-Frames (Workmat 5); 20 two-color counters; Number Cards 0–11 (Teaching Tool 12); Number Cards 12–20 (Teaching Tool 22)

Vocabulary Eleven, twelve, thirteen, fourteen, fifteen, sixteen, seventeen, eighteen, nineteen, twenty

ESL Strategies *Use before* **LEARN**   20 MIN

Focus on Meaning ➤ As you write the numbers 11, 12, 13, 14, 15, 16, 17, 18, 19, and 20 on the board, tell children they will learn more about these numbers today. Draw a large ring or box around numbers 13–19. Tell children that these seven numbers each have the same ending. Read the numbers again slowly, slightly emphasizing the *teen* part of each number name, and have children guess the ending that the numbers 13, 14, 15, 16, 17, 18, and 19 have in common. Many children will recognize that each of these numbers ends in the word *teen*. Discuss the word *teen* in relation to the word *teenagers*. Explain that the word *teen* sounds a lot like the word *ten*—but that all of the numbers you wrote on the board, including 11, 12, and 20, are greater than the number 10.

Use Manipulatives ➤ Give each child 10 counters and a set of cards for numbers 1–10. **Listen as I say a number: one.** Have each child display both the appropriate number card and the appropriate number of counters. Continue until children have had the opportunity to form the correct group of counters to match each of the number cards from 1 through 10, in ascending sequence. Then have each child use Workmat 4 to form the correct group of counters to match each number card. (Remind children to fill in the top row of the ten-frame before moving to the bottom row.)

Give each child 10 additional counters and a set of cards for numbers 11–20. Say the numbers 11–20 for children to repeat. Then have children display 11 counters by filling the ten-frame on Workmat 4 and placing one counter below the frame. Point to the ten-frame and say: **ten.** Then point to the 11th counter and say: **eleven.** Give each child Workmat 5 and have children move their 11 counters to it. Then have children show 12, 13, 14, 15, 16, 17, 18, 19, and 20, using the double ten-frames workmat. Each time have children say how many counters they are placing in the second ten-frame—and how many counters in all are in that frame.

Reading and Writing 11 and 12

ACCESS CONTENT

USE WITH LESSON 5-2

Objective Recognize and write the numerals that describe the quantities 11 and 12.

Materials Ten-Frame (Workmat 4); two-color counters; colored chalk

ESL Strategies **Use before** ▮LEARN▮ 🕐 10–15 MIN

Use Demonstration ➤ Display a ten-frame so that all children can see it. Place one counter on each frame. As you place the counters, count the numbers aloud. **One, two, . . . ten. I have 10 counters.** Then take another counter and place it below the ten-frame: **eleven. This makes 11.** Count the counters from 1 to 11 again. Then take a twelfth counter and place it next to the eleventh one. **Twelve.** Have children count the counters aloud together as you point to each one in turn.

Use Total Physical Response ➤ Tell children that they can use their bodies to make the shape of the number 11. Invite a volunteer to stand erect with his or her hands down. **This looks like the number 1.** Use your finger to trace the shape of the number next to the child's body, moving from head to toe. Then invite another child to stand next to the first one in the same fashion. Point to both children together. **This looks like the number 11. Who would like to write the number 11 on the board, using colored chalk?** Then choose a child to change the number 11 to the number 12, by changing the second 1 to a 2, using a different color of chalk.

Reading and Writing 13, 14, and 15

ACCESS CONTENT

USE WITH LESSON 5-3

Objective Recognize and write the numerals that describe the quantities 13, 14, and 15.

Materials Posterboard; large dot stickers

ESL Strategies **Use before** ▮LEARN▮ 🕐 10–15 MIN

Use Graphic Organizers ➤ Draw a ten-frame on posterboard. Fill up the first ten-frame with ten dot stickers (remembering to fill the top row in from left to right before filling in the bottom row from left to right). Count each sticker aloud as you position it. Invite children to count aloud with you. **This shows the number 10.** Put three more stickers below the ten-frame, counting each number aloud as you position the sticker that signifies that number's completion: **11, 12, 13. I added 3 more dots below my ten-frame. Now I have 13 dots in all. 10 and 3 more is 13. Let's count the 13 dots together.** Write 13 under the thirteenth dot. As you write it, say it. Then repeat for 14 and 15.

Use Total ➤
Physical Response

Have children work in pairs. Have one child stand in front of the other, with his or her back to the second child. Tell each child who is facing a partner's back to slowly "write" the number 13, 14, or 15, using a finger, on the back of the partner. **One of you writes the number, and the other one guesses the number.** Have partners switch roles, "rewriting" the numbers and giving each other hints as necessary.

Reading and Writing 16 and 17

USE WITH LESSON
5-4

ACCESS CONTENT

Objective Recognize and write the numerals that describe the quantities 16 and 17.

Materials *(per child)* Ten-Frame (Workmat 4); 20 cotton balls; 4 pieces of yarn; 2 sheets of construction paper; glue; scissors

ESL Strategies **_Use before_ LEARN**   🕐 20 MIN

Use Graphic ➤
Organizers

Remind children that they have used the ten-frame to make many numbers greater than 10. Have children brainstorm other numbers that are greater than 10. Write these numbers on the board. If children suggest the numbers 16 or 17, circle these numbers after children are done brainstorming. (If they haven't suggested them, add them to the list yourself and then circle them.) **I circled the numbers 16 and 17 because we are going to learn how to read and write these numbers.** Distribute a ten-frame and 20 cotton balls to each child. Tell children to use their ten-frames to help them count out 16 cotton balls. Circulate among children to make sure that everyone is counting correctly. Then have children repeat the process for the number 17.

Use Total ➤
Physical Response

Give each child 4 pieces of yarn, 2 sheets of construction paper, and glue. Tell children that they are going to "write" the numbers 16 and 17 with their yarn. First, demonstrate how to make the number 1 and glue it to a sheet of construction paper. (You may want to cut the yarn shorter before gluing it.) Then show children how to make the number 6. **What number do I have when I put the 1 and the 6 together, with the 1 first and then the 6?** (Allow time for children to answer. If a child answers "61," tell him or her that the number would be 61 if the 6 came first.) **I have the number 16.** Make sure both pieces of yarn are firmly glued to the paper and allow time for them to dry. Invite children to make their own "yarn numbers" for 16 and 17.

Reading and Writing 18, 19, and 20

USE WITH LESSON 5-5

ACTIVATE PRIOR KNOWLEDGE/BUILD BACKGROUND

Objective Recognize and write the numerals that describe the quantities 18, 19, and 20.

Materials 20 paper or plastic plates, cups, forks, and napkins; items for "grocery store"; play money: 20 one-dollar bills; empty grocery bag

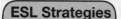
ESL Strategies

Connect to Prior Knowledge of Language ➤

Use before **LEARN**   ⏱ 20–25 MIN

Tell children that they have already learned how to read and write many numbers. Then tell them that they are going to learn how to read and write the numbers 18, 19, and 20.

Let's pretend that we are going to have a big birthday party. We have invited lots of our friends. But first we need to go shopping to get enough things for our party. Brainstorm with children some things that would probably be needed for a birthday party. Children may offer suggestions such as cake, ice cream, plates, forks, cups, and napkins. **18 people are coming to our birthday party.** Write 18 on the board. **What things will we need for each of our guests?** Help children understand that each guest will need a plate, a fork, a cup, and a napkin as well as food and a place to sit down. Set up a large table with 18 chairs around it (or create a pretend table on the floor). Have children count out with you enough place settings for the 18 guests. **Look, we have 18 plates, 18 forks, 18 napkins, and 18 cups.**

Then add 1 more of each item for the number 19 and 1 more of each item for the number 20.

Use Role Playing ➤

Have children pretend that they are shopping in a store called the "18, 19, 20 Grocery Store." Explain that in this store, there are two special rules: (1) You have to buy 18, 19, or 20 items. (2) Each item costs one dollar. Assign one child the role of clerk and two children the roles of shoppers. The first pair of shoppers should buy 18 items in all. Then they should ask the clerk, "How many things do we have in all?" With the class's help, the clerk should count the things aloud and then tell the shoppers that they have 18 items. Have the shoppers count out 18 dollars and hand them to the clerk. Finally, have the clerk bag the groceries. **Who would like to play the part of the clerk this time? Who would like to shop for 19 items?** Repeat for 20 items.

Skip Counting by 2s and 5s

USE WITH LESSON 5-6

ACTIVATE PRIOR KNOWLEDGE/ BUILD BACKGROUND

Objective Use objects and a number line to skip count by 2s and 5s.

Materials Picture of snake from magazine or book; 20 beads

Vocabulary Skip counting

ESL Strategies

Use before LEARN

 10 MIN

Connect to Prior Experiences ➤ Write a number line on the board marked from 1 to 20. **These are the numbers 1 through 20. Let's count them together.** Count slowly, pointing to each number in turn as you count.

Hold up a picture of a snake: **What is this?** *(A snake)* **Have any of you ever seen a real snake?** Allow time for children to discuss their experiences with, and knowledge of, snakes. **Snakes like to eat bugs or insects. I have 10 beads here. Let's pretend that these beads are little bugs. Do you think this snake might like to eat them? Let's count the bugs together.** Have children count each "bug" with you, from 1 to 10. Then have two volunteers arrange the 10 bugs in five groups of 2 each. With the class, model how to <u>skip count</u> the 20 bugs by 2s. Have children take turns counting by 2s independently. When children are comfortable counting by 2s, have two other volunteers rearrange the 10 bugs into two groups of 5 each. Again, count aloud and invite children to join in with you: **"5, 10. There are 10 little bugs in all."**

Then practice skip counting 20 beads by 2s and 5s.

Use Role Playing ➤ **I'm going to pretend that I'm a snake!** Cup your hands so that they look like a snake's head and make a hissing sound. Invite children to hiss with you. **I'm going to eat some bugs. I'm very, very hungry.** Slide 20 bugs in groups of 2 each near the snake (you!) and count them aloud by 2s as you pretend to eat them (perhaps by sliding them off the table into your lap). Stop at 10. **Yum, yum, yum. Now I will eat some more.** Continue in this fashion until all 20 bugs have been eaten. Invite children to role-play being snakes and practice skip counting by 2s and 5s. (You may need to remind them that it is not safe to put the counters into their mouths.)

Counting to 31

USE WITH LESSON 5-7

ACTIVATE PRIOR KNOWLEDGE/BUILD BACKGROUND; ACCESS CONTENT

Objective Use objects and ten-frames to represent and count the quantities 21 through 31.

Materials *(per child)* 31 two-color counters; 2 Double Ten-Frames (Workmat 5); Number Cards 21–31 (Teaching Tool 29); *(per group)* 1 cardboard box, containing from 21 to 31 small classroom objects, such as paper clips

ESL Strategies | *Use before* | LEARN

Connect to Prior Knowledge of Math ➤ Remind children that they have already learned to count to 20 by using their double ten-frames. Now, as you write the numbers 21–31 on the board, tell children that they will learn about the numbers 21, 22, 23, 24, 25, 26, 27, 28, 29, 30, and 31 by using *two* double ten-frames. Give each child 31 counters and 2 Double Ten-Frames. Display number cards from 21 through 31. Point to each card in turn and say each number for children to repeat. Then point to the card with 21 on it and have children display the appropriate number of counters by filling two ten-frames and then placing one counter in the upper left-hand corner of the third ten-frame. **How many counters are in your *first* ten-frame?** *(10)* **How many counters are in your *second* ten-frame?** *(10)* **How many counters are in your *third* ten-frame?** *(1)* **How many counters are there in all?** *(21)* Continue for numbers 22–31.

Give Frequent Feedback ➤ In advance, place 21, 22, 23, 24, 25, 26, 27, 28, 29, 30, or 31 small classroom objects in each group's box. Divide the class into small groups. Have children in each group use their ten-frames to determine how many objects are in their group's box. After children have placed the first ten objects in one of their ten-frames, ask: **How many objects are in your ten-frame?** *(10)* When they have filled another ten-frame with ten objects, ask: **How many objects are in both ten-frames together?** *(20)* **How many more objects do you have left over?** *(1, 2, 3, 4, 5, 6, 7, 8, 9, 10, or 11, depending on which box their group has)* **Do you have enough objects to fill your third ten-frame?** *(Yes, if there are 30 or 31 objects in all. No, if there are fewer than 30 objects in all.)*

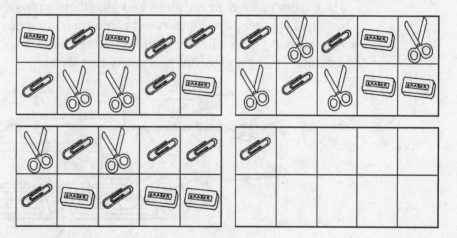

Reading and Writing Numbers Through 31

USE WITH LESSON **5-8**

ACCESS CONTENT; EXTEND LANGUAGE

Objective Recognize and write the numerals that describe the quantities 21 through 31.

Materials Shoebox; 31 two-color counters; 4 Ten-Frames (Workmat 4); *(per child)* 21–31 pipe cleaners; several cotton balls; 1 sheet of construction paper

Use Manipulatives ➤ In advance, fill a shoebox with 31 counters. Tell children that they are going to find out how many counters are in the box. Take out a ten-frame and slowly fill the first ten-frame with counters as you count from 1 to 10. Invite children to count aloud with you. Shake the box. **Do we have more counters left in the box?** *(Yes)* Tip the box so that children can see that there are a number of counters left in the box. **Do you think we can fill another ten-frame?** *(Yes)* **Yes, we need another ten-frame. Let's count together: 11, 12, 13, 14, 15, 16, 17, 18, 19, 20.** Shake the box again and tip it so that children can see inside. **Now, do you think we can fill yet another ten-frame? Why?** *(Accept all reasonable answers.)* **Let's see how many counters we have left.** Count the remaining counters aloud: **We have 11 counters left. Is this enough to fill another ten-frame? Why?** *(Yes, because 11 is more than 10)* Fill the last ten-frame and put the remaining counter below the third ten-frame (in the upper, right-hand cell of the fourth ten-frame). Then count all 31 counters, beginning with the number 1. Point to each counter as you say its number. Invite children to count along with you. Invite several volunteers to point to and count the counters independently.

Have Students ➤ **Now you are going to make creatures—creatures with many legs!**
Report Back Remind children that their creatures can look any way they choose, but that
Orally each one must have between 21 and 31 legs. Invite children to choose a number within this range. Then provide each child with the number of pipe cleaners he or she has chosen, several cotton balls, and glue. Tell children to use the cotton balls to make the body and the pipe cleaners to be the legs. Have them name their creatures and glue them to the sheets of construction paper. Have several volunteers tell about their creatures and how many legs they have. As time allows, circulate among children and help them write each creature's name and record how many legs it has.

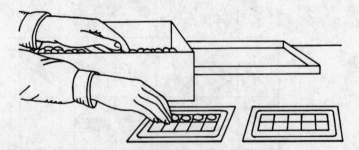

Using Estimation

ACCESS CONTENT; EXTEND LANGUAGE

USE WITH LESSON
5-9

Objective Use benchmarks to estimate the quantities of groups.

Materials *(per group)* 1 unsharpened pencil; 1 small cup of beans; 1 crayon; 1 paper clip; 1 sharpened pencil; 1 sheet of paper

Vocabulary About

Use before **LEARN**

⏱ 10–15 MIN

Use Small-Group Interactions ➤ Divide the class into small groups. Distribute an unsharpened pencil and a small cup filled with beans to each group. Explain to children that they will use some beans to estimate <u>about</u> how long an object is. Hold up your own unsharpened pencil. **Let's estimate—let's guess—about how long this pencil is. Look at one of the beans in your group's cup. Now look at your group's pencil.** *About* **how many beans do you think it will take to match the length of that pencil?** Invite children to offer suggestions and write their suggestions on the board.

Now let's find out how many beans it takes. Have children in each group mirror your actions as you use your beans to measure the approximate length of your pencil. **It takes me about (13) beans to match the length of my pencil. Has anyone found a different number?** You may need to explain that if a little bit of the pencil is left over, children should count the number of beans that comes close to matching the length of the pencil.

Have Students Report Back Orally ➤ Distribute a crayon, a paper clip, a sharpened pencil, and sheet of paper to each group. **We know that an unsharpened pencil is about 13 beans long. Do you think that a crayon is longer or shorter than a pencil?** *(Shorter)* **Yes, a crayon is shorter than a pencil. So, will we need more than 13 beans or fewer than 13 beans to measure the crayon?** *(Fewer than 13 beans)* **Yes, we will need fewer than 13 beans to measure the crayon. We know that the crayon will be fewer than 13 beans long—but how many fewer? Let's write down some of our guesses and then measure to find out.** Continue the process you followed for the pencil, writing estimates on the board, and then having each group measure to find the actual (approximate) length. Repeat the procedure with the paper clip. Have group members compare all of the objects and their corresponding "bean lengths," discussing which object is longest and which is shortest. Have group members report their findings to the class.

Comparing Numbers Through 31

ACCESS CONTENT; EXTEND LANGUAGE

USE WITH LESSON
5-10

Objective Compare two numbers to decide which is greater and which is less.

Materials Set of 10 pencils; set of 21 pencils; *(per pair)* 2 bags of cotton balls, totaling 31 in all; sheet of paper with line drawn down the middle; glue

Vocabulary Greater, less

Use before **LEARN**

⏱ 15–20 MIN

Use Real Objects ➤ Review with children the meanings of <u>greater</u> and <u>less</u>. **The number 10 is** *greater* **than the number 3. The number 3 is** *less* **than the number 10.** Invite children to create their own sentences using the words *greater* and *less*.

In one hand hold 10 pencils and in the other hand hold 21 pencils. Invite a volunteer to count the members of each set aloud. **Which hand has more** pencils? *(The hand with 21 pencils)* **How do you know?** *(Because 21 is greater than 10; because 21 pencils is more than 10 pencils)* Then continue the activity by forming two other groups of pencils. **Which group has more pencils? Which group has fewer pencils? Which number is greater? Which number is less?**

Have Students ➤ Report Back Orally

Divide the class into pairs. Give each pair of children two bags filled with cotton balls that together equal 31. (For instance, one bag might have 11 balls, and the other might have 20.) Also give each pair a sheet of paper with a line drawn down the middle. Instruct children in each pair to count the balls in one group and to write that number on one side of their paper. Then have them do the same thing with the other group. Ask children to identify which group has the *greater* number of balls, and which group has the *lesser* number. Have children glue the appropriate group of balls on each side of the paper. Then have children report their findings to the class. Invite them to explain how many balls are in each group and to tell which group has a *greater* number, and which group has *less*. If children have difficulty producing complete sentences, instruct them to point to the group that is *greater* and to say the word. Then have them do the same for *less*.

Numbers on a Calendar

USE WITH LESSON 5-11

ACTIVATE PRIOR KNOWLEDGE/BUILD BACKGROUND; ACCESS CONTENT

Objective Find, identify, and record numbers through 31 on a calendar.

Materials *(per child)* Copy of current calendar month from a real calendar; blank calendar

Vocabulary Before, after, between

ESL Strategies

Use before **LEARN**

⏱ 5–10 MIN

Connect to Prior ➤ Knowledge of Language

Show children a real calendar and flip through several pages. **What do you know about calendars?** Elicit responses from children. Ask children whether they know their birthdays and show them the dates on the calendar. Then walk through each part of a calendar, including the days, weeks, and months. Have children say "days," "weeks," and "months" aloud with you.

Distribute copies of the current calendar month. **We all have the same page from a real calendar. This page shows the month we are now in. Let's all point to the word** *(January)* **on our calendar pages.** Circulate around the class to make sure that all children are pointing to the correct word: **Let's say the name of the month together: "January."**

Distribute copies of a blank calendar. Have children write the numbers for the current month on their blank calendars: **Now let's circle today's date on our calendars.** Make sure everyone has circled the correct date. **Now I will give you some number-riddle clues. The day I am thinking of is right <u>before</u> the 6th day. Which day am I thinking of?** *(The 5th day)* **Which number should you circle?** *(The number 5)* **Now I am thinking of the day that is right <u>after</u> the 9th day. Which day am I thinking of?** *(The 10th day)* **Which number**

should you circle? (*The number 10*) **Now I am thinking of the day that is <u>between</u> the 14th day and the 16th day. Which day am I thinking of?** (*The 15th day*) **Which number should you circle?** (*The number 15*)

<table>
<tr><td>Use ➤
Peer Questioning</td><td>Divide the class into pairs and have children make up their own clues for their partners. Then invite a few volunteers to provide riddles for the class to solve.</td></tr>
</table>

Problem-Solving Strategy: Make a Table

USE WITH LESSON 5-12

EXTEND LANGUAGE; ACCESS CONTENT

Objective Solve problems by performing probability experiments and making tally marks in a table to record data.

Materials 5 pencils; (*per pair*) 1 coin; paper and pencil

Vocabulary Equally likely, more/most likely, less/least likely

ESL Strategies   ***Use before*** **LEARN**   ⏱ 15–20 MIN

Focus on Meaning ➤ **Have you ever heard of something called "tally marks"?** Make a tally mark on the board. **This is called a "tally mark." Tally marks help us count.** Have the class repeat the words with you: **"tally marks."** Explain that *tally* can also mean, "to count." **A tally mark is a mark that you make each time you count something. Each tally mark stands for 1 thing.** Show the class a set of 5 pencils and count them one by one as you record 5 tally marks on the board.

Explain that you are going to tally, or count, the number of times that a coin lands heads side up, or tails side up, after you toss it in the air. (You may need to explain that a coin has two sides. The side with the figure is called *heads*. The reverse is known as *tails*.) Draw a simple two-column table on the board with the columns labeled "Heads" and "Tails." (Use different-colored chalk for the capital *H* and the capital *T* and briefly talk about the different sounds these two letters make.)

We are going to tally each coin toss in this table that I just made. This is called a math table. Point to a table in the classroom. **This is a table with 4 legs. A math table is a different kind of table. This math table will help us keep track of the number of times this coin turns up heads or tails.**

Use Small-Group Interactions ➤ Organize children into pairs and give each pair a coin as well as a pencil and a sheet of paper. Instruct children to draw a line down the center of their papers and to write the word "Heads" (or "H") on one side, the word "Tails" (or "T")

on the other side. Then have each pair of children take turns flipping their coin. Encourage them to record a tally mark in the appropriate column each time the coin lands. After children have tossed their coins twice, ask: **If you toss the coin again, do you think it will be <u>more likely</u> or <u>less likely</u> to land on heads or tails? Or will it be <u>equally likely</u> to land on heads or tails? Why?** *(Accept all reasonable responses.)* Then have children continue tossing their coins a total of six times. Have a child from each pair present that pair's table to the class. Finally, have children make a classroom table by combining tallies from each group to record the total number of times the coins landed on heads or tails. Talk about the fact that a coin is equally likely to land on heads or tails because those are the only two ways it can land.

Problem-Solving Applications: A World of Bugs

USE WITH LESSON 5-13

ACTIVATE PRIOR KNOWLEDGE/ BUILD BACKGROUND; ACCESS CONTENT

Objective Review and apply concepts, skills, and strategies learned in this and previous chapters.

Materials 5–10 pictures of animals cut from magazines that can be easily sorted by color, size, etc.

ESL Strategies

Use before **LEARN** ⏱ 10 MIN

Connect to Prior Experiences ➤ Cut out pictures from magazines of various animals. Make sure to include several pictures of the same kind of animal, or animals with similar coloring or markings for children to sort. Hold up each picture and name it. Using descriptive words, describe the animal on the picture. Encourage children to use adjectives to describe the animal, such as "big," "brown," and so on. Also encourage children to share any information they know about the pictured animal such as "horses eat hay."

Use Pictures ➤ Then explain to children that you are going to sort the pictures. Say: **These are all animals. But I can sort them by (color).** Sort the pictures into 2 separate groups. With gestures say: **These animals are brown and these are white. Let's count the brown animals. Now let's count the white animals. What are some other ways we can sort these animals?** Provide time for children to share other ways to sort. Repeat the process of sorting pictures and counting the different groups in as many ways as possible.

Comparing and Ordering By Size

6-1

ACTIVATE PRIOR EXPERIENCES/ BUILD BACKGROUND

Objective Compare and order sets of objects by size.

Materials Goldilocks and the Three Bears; different-sized plates; cups; etc.:
3 per group

ESL Strategies   *Use before* **LEARN**   🕐 10–15 MIN

Connect to Prior ➤ Experiences

Prepare by gathering the story of Goldilocks and the Three Bears. Many books that have collections of folktales often include this popular children's story. Remember, showing children the pictures will help them to understand the story better. Another strategy to aid in comprehension is to paraphrase what happens after every few pages so that all children understand the main events. Alternatively, you may want to tell the story in simple English, showing the pictures as necessary.

How many people know the story of Goldilocks and the Three Bears? Please listen as I read (tell you) the story. As you read the story, use gestures and appropriate voices to help children visualize the meanings of the words *big*, *medium*, and *small*. **"Which bear was the biggest? Which bear was the smallest? Which bear was medium-sized?** To check comprehension, have children recount major story events.

Use Role Playing ➤

Divide children into groups. Have them pretend they are the Three Bears—Papa Bear, Mama Bear, and Baby Bear—settling down to eat after Goldilocks has left. Give them props, such as three different-sized plates, cups, and chairs.

Comparing by Length

6-2

EXTEND LANGUAGE; ACCESS CONTENT

Objective Compare objects by length.

Materials 2 sticks: 1 per child; straws; yarn

Vocabulary Longer than, shorter than, taller than, as long as (same length as), as short as, as tall as

Use before LEARN

 10–15 MIN

Focus on Language ➤ Hold up two sticks of different lengths for children to see. **This stick is longer than this stick.** Raise the longer stick. **That means that this stick is shorter than this stick. It is not as long as the first stick.** Raise the shorter stick. Explain that when two objects are not the same length, one is generally longer than the other. Explain that when we talk about people, we use the word tall to describe them, rather than long. We might say "Tony is taller than Oscar." Invite two children of different heights to the front of the class. **Who is taller? (Child A) is taller than (Child B). That means (Child B) is shorter than (Child A). Is (Child A) as tall as me? That's right, (he or she) is not. Who is (Child A) as tall as?** Invite children to the front of the class to compare their heights.

When children seem comfortable discussing these concepts, organize them into groups of 4 or 5. Give each child one full-length straw and one half-length straw. **Now hold up the straw that is longer than the other straw.** Have children put all the longer straws in the center of their work area. **Now hold up your other straw. This straw is shorter than the other straw.** Have children add the straws to the pile. Then add more full-length and half-length straws to each group's pile.

Use Total Physical Response ➤ Have each group of children sit in a circle around their pile of straws. Show children 2 lengths of yarn and place both lengths in each group's pile. Then explain the rules of the game: **One child goes first. The child sitting to his or her left goes second, and so on.** Point to one of the pieces of yarn: **Find a straw that is (shorter than or longer than) this piece of yarn.** The child should find a straw from the pile. Continue having the children retrieve different straws. When all the straws have been drawn out of a pile, the children in that group can count their straws.

Ordering by Length

USE WITH LESSON
6-3

ACCESS CONTENT

Objective Order a set of objects by length from shortest to longest.

Materials Masking tape; jars and/or bottles of various heights

Vocabulary Shortest, longest, tallest

Use before LEARN

 10–15 MIN

Use Total Physical Response ➤ Prepare by laying two different-length strips of masking tape on the floor. Make sure to leave enough room between the two strips for a third strip. Also, lay the strips in such a way so that the ends are not aligned (so it is not obvious which strip is longer.) **Can you tell which strip is longer?** Then align the strips. **Now can you tell which strip is longer? How?**

Call a volunteer forward. **Hop along the tape that is longer.** If necessary, demonstrate hopping for the class. **Slide along the tape that is shorter.**

Again, demonstrate as necessary.

Add a third strip of tape so that the three lengths of tape are in order from shortest to longest. Point to the tape that is longest. **This tape is longest.** Then point to the shortest tape. **This tape is shortest.** Again invite a volunteer forward. **Now crawl along the tape that is longest.** Demonstrate the gesture as necessary. **Tiptoe along the tape that is shortest.** Again, demonstrate the gesture as necessary. To reinforce the concepts, invite several volunteers forward to either crawl or tiptoe along the longest or shortest tape.

Which jar is shortest?

Use Real Objects ➤ Display jar and bottles of different heights. Place one of the jars or bottles on a table. Ask a child to place a jar that is shorter next to the first jar. Let that child call another child to find a third, yet shorter jar. Place this third jar next to the first two. **Which jar is shortest?** Repeat the activity several times, then ask children to find the tallest in a set of jars.

Measuring Length

USE WITH LESSON
6-4

ACCESS CONTENT

Objective Measure the length of objects using nonstandard units.

Materials Butcher paper; construction paper; yarn; tape; glue

Vocabulary Measure

ESL Strategies **Use before** LEARN ⏱ 15–20 MIN

Use ➤ **Demonstration**
Take your shoe off, hold it up, and name it. Point from one end of the shoe to the other. **I want to measure how long my shoe is. To measure is to tell how long something is.** To see how long my shoe is, I will measure the length. Length means "how long." Place the sole of your shoe on a piece of paper and trace around it. **This is a picture of my shoe. It is the same size. Now I will measure the length of the picture with this string.**

Demonstrate how to hold the string from end to end, touching the longest parts of the outline. **I'm putting the string from from the longest end to the other end. I am making the string nice and straight. Can you see how the string is touching the longest parts of the shoe from end to end? At the other end, I see that some string is left over. The string is too long. I want the string to be the same length, or just as long, as the picture of** my shoe. What can I do? (*Cut the string.*) **That's right. I need to cut the string.** Have a volunteer hold the string while you cut it. **Now the string is the same length as the picture.**

Use Small-Group ➤ Interactions

Invite children to work in pairs to measure the lengths of their shoes with string. Children can trace one of their shoes on construction paper, then measure the outline with string. Partners can help each other trace and cut as needed. Partners should ask one another: "How long is your shoe?" "Whose shoe is longer?" Have children show other children whose shoe is longer. Then have children glue all of the strings onto a classroom display, writing their names under the strings.

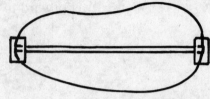

Estimating and Measuring Length

USE WITH LESSON 6-5

ACCESS CONTENT

Objective Estimate the length and width of objects and verify by measuring in nonstandard units.

Materials Masking tape; paper

Vocabulary Estimate, check

ESL Strategies | *Use before* **LEARN**

⏱ 10–15 MIN

Use ➤ Demonstration

Prepare by putting a long strip of masking tape on the floor. Then explain to children that they will use their feet to estimate the length of the tape. **Estimate means to think how many feet we'll need to match the length of this piece of tape. Look at my foot. Now look at the masking tape. If you put my foot one in front of the other, how many of your feet do you think it will take to match the length of this piece of tape?**

Have children call out estimates. **I'm going to write your estimates on the board.** Demonstrate by walking heel-to-toe along the strip. Invite the class to count aloud with you as you take each step. **It took (9) steps. Let's look back at our estimates to check how close they were.** Read each estimate aloud. Circle the estimates that are closest (or that match the actual length).

Use Total ➤ Physical Response

Divide children into small groups. Place a long strip of masking tape on the floor for each group. Have them choose a child who will measure the strip. **Look at (Child's) foot. Then look at the line.** Have children estimate by writing down how many feet they think it will take for the child to walk toe-to-heel down the strip. Have the volunteer measure the strip by walking down it. Then have children check their estimates. Have them circle a correct estimate and underline estimates closest to the actual number.

Problem-Solving Strategy: Try, Test, and Revise

ACCESS CONTENT

Objective Solve problems involving the area of shapes.

Materials Shape Outlines, (Teaching Tool 31); *(per group)* color tiles; squares and rectangles cut from construction paper

ESL Strategies | *Use before* **LEARN** | ⏱ 10 MIN

Use Demonstration

Read a big book with children that clearly shows different-shaped objects in the story. Be sure to point out several objects made of squares and rectangles, such as a window pane. Have children brainstorm any other objects they know that are made up of squares or rectangles such as a classroom door, a table, and so on.

Tape the square outline in Teaching Tool 31 to the board. Distribute copies of the outline to each child individually along with several tiles. **This is a square. It has 4 corners. Let's count the corners together.** Point to each corner as you count it aloud. **How many tiles do you think it will take to cover this square?** Write childrens' responses on the board. **These are all good guesses. Let's check your guesses. I'm going to start with the first tile and place it on top of the shape. Watch how I do this and then you try.** Make sure each child places a tile block on the square as you have done. **Now I am going to cover some more of the shape using another tile.** Make sure children are doing the same process independently. Walk around to check children's understanding. Repeat the process until the entire shape is covered. **Do you see that the entire shape is covered? How many tiles did it take for us to cover this shape? Let's count: 1, 2, 3, 4.**

Return to the estimates that children offered and read through each number. **Are there any estimates for 4?** If so, circle the number 4. If not, ask children for the numbers that are closest to the actual number. It may help to use a number line to determine numbers closest to 4. Circle the number closest to 4.

Use Small-Group Interactions

Prepare by cutting several large squares or rectangles out of construction paper. Be sure the shapes are no larger than 20 tiles each. Divide children into groups and provide each group with one of the construction paper shapes, and 20 or so tiles. Have children estimate the number of tiles it will take to cover their shape. Have them write their estimates down. Then have them work together to cover the shapes with their tiles. After they have covered their shapes, have groups count the tiles and check their estimates.

Comparing and Ordering
by Capacity

USE WITH LESSON 6-7

ACCESS CONTENT; EXTEND LANGUAGE

Objective Compare and order containers by their capacity.

Materials 3 empty different-sized boxes (such as a mint tin, sewing box, and shoe box); connecting cubes; *(per group)* 3 empty different-sized boxes; plastic balls or tennis balls

Vocabulary Empty, full, holds more, hold less, most, least

ESL Strategies   *Use before*   **LEARN**   🕐 15–20 MIN

Use Demonstration ➤ Show children two different-sized boxes such as a mint tin and sewing box. **I have two different-sized boxes. Now they are <u>empty</u>. That means there is nothing inside. If I filled them with cubes, I'm not sure which box will <u>hold more</u>. Who can tell me which box holds more?** *(The larger box)* **That's right. The larger box does hold more than the other box. That's because the sewing box is larger than the mint tin.**

Have Students Report Back Orally ➤ Put a larger box with the others, such as a shoe box. **Now if I place a third box here, which box holds the most cubes? Does anyone know what <u>most</u> means?** Encourage children to define the word most verbally or nonverbally and then restate the definition for the class if necessary. Have volunteers fill each of the three boxes with snap cubes. **Now the boxes are <u>full</u>.** Encourage children to define the word *full*, then restate its definition if necessary. Next, pour the cubes out of each box into three separate piles. Place each box behind its respective pile. Then count the cubes in each box aloud. Invite children to join in with you as you count together. Write the number of each box on an index card next to the box. Then have children explain how to order the boxes to show which box held the <u>least</u> cubes, and which box held the most.

Have groups of children order three other boxes to capacity. You might want to have children use larger items to fill the boxes, such as plastic balls or tennis balls. As children work, encourage them to discuss the ordering process with one another. Visit each group and have group members explain their conclusions as to which box held the most, held the least, or why they ordered their boxes the way they did.

Estimating and Measuring Capacity

USE WITH LESSON 6-8

ACCESS CONTENT

Objective Estimate and measure capacity using nonstandard units.

Materials Pitcher filled with water; cups; large bowl; *(per group)* containers for noodles or pasta; cups; bowls; paper; dry pasta noodles

Use before LEARN

🕐 10 MIN

Use Real Objects ➤ Show children one of the drinking cups they typically use during snack time. Then show them a half-gallon pitcher filled with water and name it. You may want to point out that the word *pitcher* sounds a lot like the word *picture*. Explain that English has many words that sound alike, but that have different meanings. Explain the meanings of these words.

Point to the cup. **How many times do you think I could fill this cup with water from this pitcher?** Have children offer their estimates and write them on the board. **Let's check your predictions.** Have a volunteer pour the pitcher of water into the cup, then empty the cup of water into a large bowl. Make tally marks on the board each time the cup is filled.

When the pitcher has been emptied, count the tally marks together. Look back at children's predictions and circle the estimate that is correct. Underline the estimates that are closest to the actual number.

Use Small-Group ➤ Divide children into small groups. Give each group a large container filled
Interactions with dry pasta noodles, a cup, and a large bowl. Make sure each group's container is filled to different capacities. Have each child in the group first say and then write his or her estimate of how many cups of noodles are in the container. Then have them check their estimates by working together to pour the noodles into the cup. When finished, have children circle any correct estimates and underline the two estimates that are closest. Provide a number line for children's use to help them determine the closest numbers. Finally, have children discuss their findings with the class. If they have difficulty using full sentences, invite them to share the numbers of their predictions and then the actual number.

Comparing and Ordering by Weight

USE WITH LESSON
6-9

ACCESS CONTENT

Objective Compare and order objects by weight.

Materials Balance scale; 2 pencils; eraser; toy car; hardcover book; *(per group)* 3 classroom objects of different weights

Vocabulary Heavier (weighs more), lighter (weighs less), about the same

Use before LEARN

🕐 10–15 MIN

Use ➤ Show children a balance scale. Explain that scales weigh things. **This is a**
Demonstration **balance scale. There are two sides. When two objects are put on the scale (one on each side), the scale will show which object is <u>heavier</u> and which object is <u>lighter</u>.** *Heavier* **means weighs more and** *lighter* **means weighs less. However when objects are <u>about the same</u>, the scale will not tip to one side or the other; it will move, but eventually stay in the middle.** Demonstrate by putting one pencil on each side of the scale, pointing out that the pencils weigh about the same.

Hold up a pencil eraser and small toy car. **I'm going to place this eraser on one side of the scale. See how the scale goes down a little bit? Now I'm going to place this toy car on the other side. Do you think that the scale will show that the car is heavier or lighter than the eraser?** Place the car on the scale. **Look! The car is heavier than the eraser. We can tell because the side of the scale holding the car went down lower than the side holding the eraser.**

Use
Graphic Organizers ➤

Write "heavier" on one side of the board and "lighter" on the other side. **I will draw a toy car on this side of the board, under the word *heavier*, because the car was heavier than the eraser. I'll draw an eraser on this side under the word *lighter* because the eraser is lighter than the car. Now let's weigh one more object and compare it to the two we've already weighed.** Show children a hardcover book and name it. Repeat the process using the book and eraser. Have children tell you where you should draw the book on the board to show how its weight compares to the weight of the eraser, then the car.

Estimating and Measuring Weight

USE WITH LESSON
6-10

ACTIVATE PRIOR KNOWLEDGE/BUILD BACKGROUND

Objective Estimate the weight of objects and measure their weight in nonstandard units.

Materials Picture of seesaw; balance scale; common objects for weighing such as branch, feather, pencil, block, play food; connecting cubes

Vocabulary Balance, weight

ESL Strategies

Use before LEARN

 15–20 MIN

Connect to Prior
Experiences ➤

Show children a picture of a seesaw. Ask them about their experiences of playing on a seesaw. You may want to use hand gestures to show the motion that a seesaw makes as it goes up and down. **We've used a <u>balance</u> scale before. Did you know that a balance scale is a lot like a seesaw? Can anyone tell me how? What happens on a seesaw when one side goes down?** With children, gesture how a seesaw moves.

Now we are going to use our balance scale as we weigh some objects. Have at your disposal several cubes and items to weigh such as a branch, feather, pencil, block, play food. Have children "measure" with their hands the block and one cube. **Which is heavier?** *(The block)* Put a block on one side of the scale. Point out to children how the weight of the object made the scale go down. **We are going to see how many cubes it will take to make the scale sides balance.** Demonstrate the meaning of *level*. Slowly place cubes on the opposite side. Count each cube as you place it. **Let's see how many cubes it took to equal the <u>weight</u> of the block.** Count them aloud. Repeat the activity with a pencil, branch, feather, and play food.

Temperature

ACTIVATE PRIOR EXPERIENCES/BUILD BACKGROUND; ACCESS CONTENT

Objective Investigate temperature using comparative words and identity the thermometer as a tool for measuring temperature.

Materials Thermometer; pictures from magazines of outdoor scenes and people; wearing clothing for cold or hot weather; constuction paper; glue

Vocabulary Warmer, cooler, hotter, colder, thermometer

ESL Strategies

Use before **LEARN**

 10–15 MIN

Connect to Prior Knowledge of Language ➢ Show children a <u>thermometer</u>. Explain that a thermometer tells the temperature, or how hot or cold it is outside. Point out that the temperature can be read in numbers. A high number means that it's hot while a low number means that it's cold. Ask children to share any experiences they may have had with thermometers. **What do you like to do in <u>hotter</u> weather?** *(Swimming, going to the beach)* **What do you like to do in <u>colder</u> weather?** *(Skiing, sledding)* Children may also want to share experiences and weather in their countries of origin.

Hold up a thermometer. **Have any of you seen one of these before? Where was it?** *(Outside)* Write the number 80 on the board. **If it's 80 degrees outside, that means it's pretty warm. What are some clothes you wear when its warm outside?** *(Shorts, t-shirts, sandals, sunglasses)* Write 30 on the board. **If it's 30 degrees outside, that means its pretty cold. What are some clothes you where when its cold outside?** *(Sweaters, jackets, scarves, mittens, gloves, coats, boots)*

You may want to explain what happens to an adjective, or describing word, when the ending *–er* is added. Explain that the ending can change the meaning of the word. It can act as a superlative, as when comparing two things: "It is <u>cooler</u> today than yesterday." Or, it can be used idiomatically as in "I like cooler weather." Have children discuss the meanings of the other words: <u>warmer</u>, hotter, colder. Encourage them to use them in sentences.

Use Pictures ➢ Give children the pictures of cold-and hot-weather outdoor scenes and people; construction paper and glue. Have each child decide if he or she will make a hot- or cold-weather collage. When children are finished, have them talk briefly about their collages.

Problem-Solving Application: Around the Home

ACCESS CONTENT

Objective Review and apply concepts, skills, and strategies learned in this and previous chapters.

Materials Bowl filled with breakfast cereal; 3 containers including a larger bowl (such as a mixing bowl); spoon; cup; measuring cup

Use before **LEARN**

Use Real Objects ➤ Fill a bowl with breakfast cereal. Have 3 or more other containers including a larger bowl, a spoon, a cup, and a measuring cup on hand. Gesturing to the bowl filled with cereal. **This bowl is cracked. It will not hold milk. I need to pour my cereal into another container.** Pick up each container and name it. Use descriptive words to describe the containers, such as "deep," "round" "shallow," and so on. Encourage children to join in with their own observations about the containers.

Use Graphic ➤ Draw a chart with 4 columns. Draw a picture of each container (the larger
Organizers bowl, the spoon, the cup, and the measuring cup) at the top of each column.
Which container do you think will hold all the cereal in this bowl? Invite children to raise their hands if they think the cereal will fit into the larger bowl, the spoon, and so on. Tally the predictions into your chart. **It looks like more children think the cereal will fit into (the larger bowl).** Demonstrate your reasoning by circling the number and explaining that it is the largest of the four predictions. Then have a volunteer pour the bowl of cereal into each container. **Which container did the cereal fit into?** *(The larger bowl)* **What happened when the cereal was poured into the other containers, such as the spoon?** *(It spilled out.)* Help children to order the containers from smallest to largest.

Days of the Week

EXTEND LANGUAGE; ACCESS CONTENT

USE WITH LESSON
7-1

Objective Identify and order the days of the week.

Materials Calendar; multiple sets of 7 index cards each, labeled with the 7 days of the week (enough for each child to have 1 card)

Vocabulary Days of the week

ESL Strategies | *Use before* **LEARN** | ◔ 15 MIN

Focus on Meaning ➤ Point out the <u>days of the week</u> on a calendar. **These are the days of the week. Who knows how many days are in a week? Let's count them.** Write the days of the week in order (starting with Sunday) on the board. Have the class say the days aloud with you as you point to each one in turn. Model counting the days off with your fingers as you say them aloud. **How many days is that?** *(7)* **Yes, there are 7 days in a week. On some days, we come to school. On some days we don't. What day of the week comes first?** Point to Sunday. **Do we come to school on Sunday?** *(No)* **What day comes second?** Point to Monday. **Do we come to school on Monday?** *(Yes)* Continue through Saturday, using ordinals as well as the days' names. **Again, how many days are there in a week?** *(7)* Have the class say the days of the week aloud with you as you point to each one in turn.

Use Total ➤ **We can make a parade of the days of the week.** Pass out all of the cards at
Physical Response random. **Who has Sunday? Who has Monday?** Continue with all the days until everyone in the class has answered. **Okay, Sundays, you line up first, right here. Now, Mondays, you line up second, next to Sunday's line.** Continue to line the children up in the order of the days of the week until you have 7 separate lines. Have all children hold up their cards. Then have the 7 lines become one line as you parade around the room. **When I say "Sunday," the Sundays will cheer, "Hooray!" and start marching around the room. Then, when I say "Monday," the Mondays will cheer, "Hooray!" and get in line behind the Sundays.** Continue through all the days until the parade has completed one or two circuits around the classroom. Then have children return to their seats. Finally, collect the cards by having children bring them up to you in order.

Yesterday, Today, and Tomorrow

ACCESS CONTENT

Objective Identify yesterday, today, and tomorrow.

Materials *(per group)* 3 simple signs (see illustration below); tape

Vocabulary Yesterday, today, tomorrow

ESL Strategies *Use before* **LEARN** 10–15 MIN

Use Pantomime ➤ Have groups of children play Charades using the terms <u>yesterday</u>, <u>today</u>, and <u>tomorrow</u>. Place the signs, one for each word, in order on the chalk tray. Have children read the signs aloud with you. Stand by the first sign. **I'm standing next to the yesterday card because I am going to act out something I did yesterday.** Pantomime an action such as throwing a ball. **Can you tell what I'm doing?** *(Throwing a ball)* **Let's say I did this yesterday. What did I do yesterday? Say it with me: "Yesterday I threw a ball."** Move to the "today" card. Repeat the process with another pantomimed action, such as petting a dog. Encourage children who are able to do so, to describe the activity using a complete sentence, such as "Today I am petting a dog." Move to the "tomorrow" card and pantomime an activity such as dancing. **What will I do tomorrow?** *(Tomorrow you will dance.)* Move back to the "yesterday" card and review the process, both physically and verbally. Help children recognize that the first action happened before today and the third action will happen after today.

Use Small-Group Interactions ➤ Have children work in small groups. **Now it's your turn to play Charades.** Pass out the signs and tape to each group. **Make sure you put up the signs in order. Which sign goes before the one that says "today"? Which sign goes after the one that says "today"?** Have groups take turns acting out activities they took part in yesterday and today and activities they will (or might) take part in tomorrow. Children should stand in front of the appropriate card as they act out each activity. **After you guess what the activity is, say it in a sentence.** Circulate among groups and have children explain their activity to you using the vocabulary words in complete sentences, as they are able.

Months and Seasons

ACCESS CONTENT

Objective Name the months and seasons of the year.

Materials Calendar with pictures; crayons; paper

Vocabulary Month, year, season

ESL Strategies   *Use before* **LEARN**   🕐 15–20 MIN

Use Real Objects ➤ Show children a calendar. **This is a calendar. Each page shows a different <u>month</u>.** Count the months aloud with children as you flip through them. Make sure children understand that there are 12 months in a <u>year</u>. **Let's see if we can name all 12 months in the year. Who can tell me the name of a month?** Write the name of each month in vertical order on the board, filling in the months that children do not call out. Then have children recite the months in order with you. Recite the months one at a time, asking children to raise their hands if that month is their birthday month.

Use Pictures ➤ Flip through the calendar pictures. **What does this picture show? It's a picture of winter. And what do these pictures show?** *(Spring, summer, fall)* Write each <u>season's</u> name on the board, next to the months that are in that season. **Winter, spring, summer, and fall are called the seasons of the year.** Have children recite them and count them with you. **How many seasons are there?** *(4)* Ask children to talk about the weather and outdoor activities associated with each season where you live, producing sentences such as: "It's cool in the fall;" "You rake leaves in fall;" "It's hot in the summer;" "You have picnics in the summer."

Pass out crayons and paper. **Draw a picture for any season you want.** Give children some examples. **You could draw a swimming pool for summer or a flower for spring.** Ask volunteers to show their pictures and to name the seasons their pictures represent. Ask children to guess what month might be appropriate for each picture that is presented.

Calendar

ACCESS CONTENT

Objective Identify the different parts of a calendar.

Materials Enlargement or drawing of real calendar page for current month; crayons; *(per child)* copy of same calendar page

Vocabulary Date, day, calendar

Use before **LEARN** 🕐 15–20 MIN

Use Real Objects ➤ Display the enlarged or drawn calendar for the current month. **Review what a <u>calendar</u> is.** Review each part as you point to it: <u>day</u>, week, month. **How many days are in a week?** *(7)* **How many months are in a year?** *(12)*

Pass out copies of the calendar page. **This calendar page shows this month—the month we're right now. What month are we in right now?** Make sure children know what month it is. Repeat the name of the month aloud with them. Have them draw a ring around the name of the month on the calendar page. **Let's find all of the days of the week.** Have children underline the days of the week in order with 7 different-colored crayons as you underline them on the displayed calendar. **Let's draw a green line under the word** *Monday.* (And so on.) **What else is on the calendar? What are all of these numbers?** Have children read the numbers aloud with you, 1 through 31. Have children talk about what the numbers might mean.

Let's look at our calendar again. I want to find today's <u>date</u> on the calendar. What day is today? Encourage responses from children. **Yes, today is (February 10).** Point to that date on the displayed calendar. Have children circle today's date on their calendars in red. Walk around the room to make sure that all children are using their red crayons to circle the correct date.

Tell children to mark an *X* on the day before. **(February 10) is today. So what date was it yesterday?** *(February 9)* **You can check the numbers. You know that 9 comes before 10. So (February 9) is the day before (February 10).** Mark the day on the enlarged calendar with an *X*. Repeat the process for the day before that, and so on, until children have crossed out all of the days before the current with *X*'s. Make sure they understand that each date falls on a certain day.

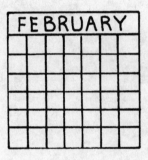

Ordering Events

USE WITH LESSON
7-5

ACTIVATE PRIOR KNOWLEDGE/BUILD BACKGROUND; ACCESS CONTENT

Objective Decide the order in which a sequence of events occurs.

Materials *(per group)* 3 simple signs

Vocabulary First, next, last, before, after

Use before **LEARN** 🕐 15–20 MIN

Use Literature ➤ Begin by reminding children that in a story something happens <u>first</u>, or at the beginning of a story. Then something happens <u>next</u> or <u>after</u> that. And then something happens <u>last</u>, at the end of the story. You may want to illustrate this point by retelling a familiar story such as "The Three Little Bears." Be sure to also review with children the concepts of <u>before</u> and <u>after</u> as you discuss the story.

Place each of the 3 signs in order on the chalk tray. Have children read them aloud with you. **I am going to act out something we all do every day.** Pantomime brushing your teeth. **What am I doing?** *(Brushing teeth)* **Now I'm going to show how I brush my teeth.** Stand near the first sign and pantomime putting toothpaste on a toothbrush. **First I put toothpaste on my toothbrush.** Move to the second sign. **What I do next, or after I put toothpaste on my toothbrush?** Pantomime brushing your teeth. **Yes! Next I brush my teeth!** Move to the last sign. **What I do last?** Pantomime rinsing your mouth out. **Yes, I rinse out my mouth.** Review the process, both physically and verbally. Then up the order so that children have to tell you what you do first, before you rinse out your mouth, what you do next, after you put toothpaste on your toothbrush, and so on.

**Use Small-Group ➤
Interactions**

Have small groups of children take turns acting out the first, next, and last steps involved in getting ready for school. Children should step from one card to the next as they act out each step in the process. Encourage children who are describing the actions to use the words *first, next,* and *last.*

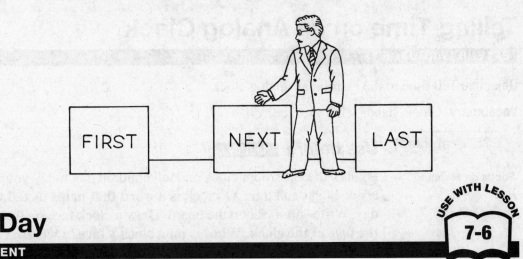

Time of Day

ACCESS CONTENT

USE WITH LESSON
7-6

Objective Identify the time of day as day or night; morning, afternoon, or evening

Materials Simple time-line illustrations (see below)

Vocabulary Day, night, morning, afternoon, evening

ESL Strategies   ***Use before*** **LEARN**   🕐 10–15 MIN

**Use ➤
Graphic Organizers**

Write a simple "time line" of a day on the board. Discuss the time line with children, pointing to each section as you name it. **These are the parts that make up our <u>day</u>.** Have children say the words with you: "**<u>Morning</u>, <u>afternoon</u>, <u>evening</u>, and <u>night</u>.**" Point to each part as you discuss it with children. **The morning is the first part of our day. What do you do in the morning?** *(Wake up, get ready for school, eat breakfast, wait for the bus)* **The next part of our day is the afternoon. The afternoon part of our day begins around the time we eat lunch. What are some things that we do in the afternoon?** *(Eat lunch, go home from school, play)* Discuss *evening* and *night* in the same manner.

Now I will name and act out an activity, and then I'd like someone to tell me whether that activity happens in the morning, the afternoon, the evening, or at night. Ask volunteers to come up to the board and point to the correct section of the time line. Use each of their answers in a sentence. Have children repeat the sentences with you as they are able.

Morning	Afternoon	Evening	Night

Telling Time on an Analog Clock

EXTEND LANGUAGE

USE WITH LESSON
7-7

Objective Tell time to the hour on an analog clock.

Vocabulary Clock, hands, o'clock, face

ESL Strategies

Use before LEARN

🕐 10–15 MIN

Focus on Meaning ➤ Point to the classroom clock and tell children that today you are going to talk about <u>clocks</u> and time. **O'clock is a word that helps us tell the hour of the day.** Write "o'clock" on the board. Draw a clock face on the board. **This is the <u>face</u> of the clock. What is on a clock's face?** *(Numbers and hand)* As children tell you the things that are on a clock face, draw them on your clock face. **How many numbers are there?** *(12)* Starting with the 1 on the clock, point to each hour in turn and read each number with children followed by the word *o'clock*. Then draw the <u>hands</u> of the clock. **These are the hands of the clock. Show me your hands. How many hands do you have?** *(2)* **How many hands does a clock have?** *(2)* Explain that the short hand tells the hour and the long hand tells the minutes.

Tell children what time you wake up in the morning. **I wake up at 6 o'clock in the morning. Where would I put the hands of the clock to show what time I wake up in the morning?** Erase the clock hands and then redraw them to show the hour that you just named. Ask for volunteers to tell what the class might be doing at certain times of the school day. Redraw the clock hands to show each of these times.

Focus on Use ➤ Help children use sentences with *o'clock* in them by recasting those statements to include a time on the hour. **(Child A) eats breakfast at 7 o'clock on school**

mornings. What time does school start? That's right, school starts at 8 o'clock. 8 o'clock is one hour after (Child A) wakes up.

Telling Time on a Digital Clock

USE WITH LESSON 7-8

ACCESS CONTENT

Objective Tell time to the hour on a digital clock.

Materials Analog clock and digital clock

Vocabulary Digital clock

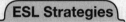 **ESL Strategies**   *Use before*   **LEARN**   🕐 15–20 MIN

Use Real Objects ➤ Show children an analog clock set to 4 o'clock. **This clock shows 4 o'clock. How do we know this?** *(The short hand points to 4; the long hand points to 12.)* Show children a <u>digital clock</u> also set to 4 o'clock. **This is called a digital clock. Have any of you seen this type of clock before?** Encourage children to use the words digital clock in their answers. **This digital clock also says 4 o'clock. The 4 is showing next to these two dots and two zeros, and the two dots and two zeros mean o'clock.** Change the time on the digital clock to show 8 o'clock. **What time does this digital clock show now?** *(8 o'clock)* **How do you know?** Guide children through telling different times on the digital clock until they are comfortable. Ask a volunteer to tell you what time to change the clock to. **Can anyone tell me how to set it for that time?**

Use Gestures ➤ Change the analog clock again and then the digital clock to show the same hour. Have children tell you whether the times are the same. *(Yes)* Change them to show different hours. Have children tell you whether the times are the same. *(No)* **How can I change the digital clock to show the correct time?** Have children use gestures indicating up or down until you have the clock set to the right time. Repeat the process for other times and then have children gradually take over. Ask pairs of volunteers to come up: one to change the digital clock, one to change the analog clock. Have them display the clocks and explain what they are doing to the rest of the class.

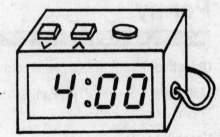

More Time and Less Time

USE WITH LESSON 7-9

ACCESS CONTENT

Objective Identify the activity or event that takes more time or less time.

Vocabulary More time, less time

Use before LEARN

⏱ 10–15 MIN

**Use Total ➤
Physical Response**

Tell children that they are going to talk about how some activities take longer to do than other activities. Then have them stand up and join hands. Point to the right. **Let's all take 2 steps. Ready? 1 step . . . 2 steps. Now sit down.** Then have children stand up again. **Now we're going to walk all the way around the circle 2 times and then sit down.** Have children join hands and lead them twice around in a circle. Then have them sit down. **Did it take <u>more time</u> to walk around 2 circles than it took to walk 2 steps?** *(Yes)*

**Use Small-Group ➤
Interactions**

For the next activity, group children together. Make each group as large as possible. Have one group come forward. **Touch your noses.** When group members touch their noses, clap once. **Now take 10 giant steps.** As children take their 10 giant steps, count the steps aloud and clap once for each step. Make sure all children have had a turn to participate. **Did it take <u>less time</u> to touch your noses than it took to walk 10 giant steps?** *(Yes)* **Some things take more time, and some things take less time.** Ask children to give you some reasons that some things take more time and some things take less time.

Continue to compare and contrast situations that take more time and less time. **Which would take more time, clapping your hands once or eating a great big bowl of soup?** *(Eating a bowl of soup)* **Which would take less time, closing a door or climbing a mountain?** *(Closing a door)*

Penny

USE WITH LESSON
7-10

Objective Recognize a penny and identify the value of a given set of pennies.

Materials *(per child)* 4 pennies; circles cut from construction paper for "pennies"; markers

Vocabulary Penny, cent, cent sign

Use before LEARN

⏱ 15–20 MIN

Use Real Objects ➤

Give each child a <u>penny</u>. **Does anyone know what these are?** *(Pennies)* **What could you use pennies for?** *(To buy something)* **Look at your penny and tell me something about it. What color is it? Is there a picture on it? Are there numbers?**

Hold up 1 penny. Tell children that 1 penny is worth 1 <u>cent</u>. Write "1¢" on the board. **This number is read like this: "one cent."** Point to the cent sign. **This symbol is called a <u>cent sign</u>.** Then give each child three additional pennies. Write "3¢" on the board. Model how to count 3 pennies: **1 cent, 2 cents, 3 cents. 3 pennies are worth 3¢.** Then write "2¢" on the board and ask a child to come forward and show 2¢. **1 cent, 2 cents: 2 pennies are worth 2¢.** Write "1¢" on the board: **Show 1¢ with your pennies.** Continue until children have practiced showing 1¢, 2¢, 3¢, and 4¢ with their pennies. Each time have children repeat the model sentence with you: **"(2) pennies are worth (2) cents."**

Use Total Physical Response ➤ Have children make their own "pennies." Give each child a circle cut out of brown construction paper. Have children each draw a picture of themselves on one side. On the opposite side, have them draw a picture of home or school. When all children have completed their "pennies," have them discuss what they drew. Display the "pennies" around the class.

Nickel

ACTIVATE PRIOR KNOWLEDGE/BUILD BACKGROUND

USE WITH LESSON 7-11

Objective Identify a nickel and its value; find the value of a nickel and some pennies.

Materials *(per child)* 5 pennies and 1 nickel; 4 classroom toys and 4 index cards, each labeled 5¢

Vocabulary Nickel

ESL Strategies

Connect to Prior Knowledge of Math ➤

Use before **LEARN**   🕐 10–15 MIN

Tell children that they will learn about <u>nickels</u>. Hold up 1 nickel. Tell children that 1 nickel is worth 5¢. Give each child a nickel and have children look at both sides of their coins. **What can you tell me about the nickels you are holding?** Give each child 5 pennies and ask children to place the nickel in one group and the pennies in another group. **Point to your pennies. Now point to your nickel.** Check to make sure that all children are pointing to the correct coins. Then have them count their nickels and tell you how many they have. *(1)* Have them count their pennies and tell you how many they have. *(5)* **How much money are your 5 pennies worth?** *(5¢)* **How much money is your 1 nickel worth?** *(5¢)*

Place 4 classroom toys on a table and name them. Place an index card labeled 5¢ in front of each toy. Point to one of the toys. **How many pennies would you need to buy this toy?** *(5)* **How many nickels would you need to buy this toy?** *(1)*

Use Role Playing ➤ Then invite a child to choose a toy to "buy." **This toy costs 5¢. Will you buy it with 1 nickel or 5 pennies?** When the child decides whether to

use the nickel or the 5 pennies, take the coin or coins and give him or her the toy. Continue in this manner until all four of the toys have been "bought" with coins. Repeat with four new volunteers.

Dime

USE WITH LESSON
7-12

ACTIVATE PRIOR KNOWLEDGE/BUILD BACKGROUND

Objective Identify a dime and its value; find the value of a given set of coins.

Materials *(per child)* 1 dime and 10 pennies

Vocabulary Dime

ESL Strategies

Use before **LEARN** 🕐 10–15 MIN

Connect to Prior ➤
Knowledge of
Math

Hold up 1 <u>dime</u>. Tell children that 1 dime is worth 10¢. Give each child a dime and have children look at both sides of their coins. **What can you tell me about the dimes you are holding?** After children have looked at and discussed their dimes, give each child 10 pennies. Have children place the coins in front of them in two groups: the penny group and the dime group. Ask children to point to their pennies and then to their dimes. Have them each count their dimes and tell you how many they have. *(1)* Have them each count their pennies and tell you how many they have. *(10)* **How much money are your 10 pennies worth?** *(10¢)* **How much money is your 1 dime worth?** *(10¢)*

Problem-Solving Strategy: Act It Out

USE WITH LESSON
7-13

ACTIVATE PRIOR KNOWLEDGE/BUILD BACKGROUND; ACCESS CONTENT

Objective Solve problems using coins to act out purchasing situations and show prices in different ways.

Materials Toys, trinkets, and books with price labels between 1¢ and 10¢ each; signs listing items and prices; *(per child)* supply of play pennies, nickels, and dimes from classroom coin set

ESL Strategies

Use before **LEARN** 🕐 15–20 MIN

Connect to Prior ➤
Knowledge of
Math

Display the assortment of items on shelves and tables to look like a store. Organize the toys into four or five separate stations. Label each item with a price. Review the value and name of each coin as you write its name on the board. **How much is a penny worth?** (Next to the word *penny,* draw a circle with "1¢" written inside the circle.) **How much is a nickel worth?** (Next to the word *nickel,* draw a circle with "5¢" written inside the circle.) **How much is a dime worth?** (Next to the word *dime,* draw a circle with "10¢" written inside the circle.) **Now you will use pennies, nickels, and dimes to buy presents for your friends!** Explain that they will take turns shopping and selling.

Use ➤
Role Playing

Invite a volunteer to help you demonstrate how to buy something. **I have a friend who likes (necklaces). I would like to buy one for her. I have some**

coins here. Show children how you count the coins. Begin to "shop," talking about various items and prices. Then turn to the volunteer and say: **I want to buy this (necklace) for (8 cents). Here are (1 nickel and 3 pennies).** Help the seller count the money aloud, touching first the nickel and then each of the three pennies in turn: **"5 cents, 6 cents, 7 cents, 8 cents."** Next have a volunteer demonstrate how to make a purchase from another child. Encourage children to discuss the transaction and name the coins they are using.

Use Small-Group ➤ Interactions

Have a small group work at each station. Half the group will sell while the other half purchases. Then have children switch roles. As you circulate, ask each child what he or she bought or sold and how much the item cost. Encourage children to use complete sentences as they are able.

Quarter and Dollar

USE WITH LESSON 7-14

ACTIVATE PRIOR KNOWLEDGE/BUILD BACKGROUND

Objective Identify a quarter and its value; identify a dollar bill.

Materials Art supplies with price labels of 25¢ or $1.00; (per child) 2 Dollar Bills (Teaching Tool 38); 5 quarters from classroom set

Vocabulary Quarter, dollar, dollar sign

ESL Strategies

Connect to Prior ➤ Knowledge of Math

Use before **LEARN**   🕐 15–20 MIN

Group and place art supplies in several different bins and assign them prices of 25 cents or $1.00. Tell children that they are going to learn about <u>quarters</u> and <u>dollars</u> as they buy supplies in the "store."

You learned about pennies, nickels and dimes. Now you will learn about quarters and dollars. On the board, draw a circle to represent a quarter and write "25¢" inside the circle. Show children a quarter and pass it around. Have them describe a quarter. Then hold up a dollar. **This is a dollar. How is it different from a quarter?** *(It is made of paper; it is not a coin.)* Have children describe the dollar. Then write "$" on the board. Point out to children that the <u>dollar sign</u> comes before the amount, while the cent sign comes after the amount.

Use Role Playing ➤

Tell children that they will have an opportunity to buy art supplies. Provide each child with 2 dollars and 5 quarters. Tell children they can spend their money in the store any way they want. Role-play being the clerk and have children "buy" art supplies from you, using their money. Encourage them to count their money aloud as they make their purchases. Once children have bought their supplies, invite them to use them to create a picture.

Comparing Values

ACCESS CONTENT

USE WITH LESSON 7-15

Objective Compare the values of individual coins and combinations of coins through 10¢.

Materials Index cards with combinations of coins amounting to less than 10 cents taped to each

ESL Strategies | *Use before* **LEARN** | ⏱ 15–20 MIN

Use Real Objects ➤ Tape 5 pennies onto one index card and 1 nickel and 2 pennies on another card. On the board, make a chart that shows the value of a penny, a nickel, and a dime. Read the chart aloud. Then model for children how to count the coins on the two index cards as you count them aloud: **"1¢, 2¢, 3¢, 4¢, 5¢."** (Write "5¢" on the accompanying card.) **"5¢, 6¢, 7¢."** (Write "7¢" on the accompanying card.) Hold the cards in separate hands. **Which card is worth more money?** Have children point to the card with more money. **This card has 5 coins on it, and this card has only 3 coins on it. But 7 cents is more than 5 cents.** Invite children to join you in recounting each set. Repeat this process again with two cards showing different values, each less than 10 cents.

Use Small Group Interactions ➤ Provide small groups with two index cards with coin values under 10 cents each. Have children count the coins together. Then have them discuss which card has more money, and which has less money. Invite them to use English as they count the cards and reach their conclusions. For instance, "This card has 4 cents. This card has 6 cents. The card with 6 cents has more money." If children are not ready to use complete sentences, encourage them to indicate the amount on each card. Then have them tell which card is worth more and which card is worth less.

Problem-Solving Applications: Time to Play

ACCESS CONTENT

Objective Review and apply key concepts, skills, and strategies learned in this and previous chapters.

Materials *(per group)* Index card with a time, such as 7:00, written on it—a different time for each group

ESL Strategies   *Use before* **LEARN**   🕐 15–20 MIN

Use Pantomime ➤ Tell children they are going to pantomime things that happen throughout the day. On the board, write "8:00." **I've written 8:00 on the board. Look at what I'm doing.** Pantomime driving your car. **I am driving my car. This is what I do at 8:00 in the morning. I drive my car to school. What do you do at 8:00 in the morning?** Many children will remark that they go to school at this time as well. **How do you go to school?** Children may respond that they walk, or take the bus, or ride a bike. Invite children to pantomime how they go to school.

Write "12:00" on the board and say the time aloud. Pantomime eating lunch. **At 12:00, I eat my lunch. That is what I do almost every day at this time. What do you do at 12:00 in the afternoon?** Accept all reasonable answers and have children pantomime their activities at 12:00. Continue in this manner with other times throughout the day.

Use Small-Group Interactions ➤ Divide the class into small groups. Distribute an index card with a time written on it to each group. Have the groups pantomime activities that they do at this time. Before they pantomime, however, have them discuss among themselves the activities that they do at this time.

Solid Figures

USE WITH LESSON

8-1

ACCESS CONTENT

Objective Identify spheres, cubes, cones, cylinders.

Materials Square block; ball; can of soup; conical party hat; construction-paper circle sized to function as a flat surface for the hat

Vocabulary Cube, sphere, cylinder, cone

ESL Strategies

Use before **LEARN**

 10–15 MIN

Use Real Objects ➤ Point out a common, three-dimensional solid figure, such as a filing cabinet, in the classroom. **Everywhere you look, you can find solid figures. Some of them have flat parts. Some of them have round parts.** Invite children to point out other solid figures, such as a globe, in the classroom. Hold up the square block. **Can anyone tell me what this is?** *(A block)* **Let's look at the shape of this block. Are the 6 sides different, or are they the same?** Guide children to see that the 6 sides of the block are all the same size and shape. **This block is also called a <u>cube</u>.** Have children repeat the word *cube* with you. **A cube has 6 sides that are all the same size and shape.** Pass the cube around.

Expand Student ➤ Show children the ball. Ask them how they know that it's a ball. *(It's round.)*
Responses **Yes, a ball is round. And a ball is also called a <u>sphere</u>.** Have children repeat the word *sphere* with you. Turn the ball over in your hands. **What can we say about this sphere?** Have children make their own observations (e.g., it doesn't have any flat parts). Pass the sphere around.

Show children the can of soup. **What's this?** *(A can)* Turn the can over in your hands. **Is this can as round as the ball?** *(No; parts of the can are not round.)* Ask children to tell you what part of the can is round and what parts of the can are flat. **If a shape is round, and it has 2 flat parts that are opposite each other, it is called a <u>cylinder</u>.** Have children repeat the word *cylinder* with you. Pass the can around.

Hold up the conical-shaped party hat. **This party hat is shaped a little bit like a <u>cone</u>. Now, if we put a flat bottom on the hat** (hold the construction-paper circle against the bottom of the hat), **then it really does look like a cone because it looks solid.** Have children repeat the word *cone* with you. **A cone has one curved part, one flat side, and one point.** Ask volunteers to come up and point to the curved surface, the flat side (the base), and the point. Have children compare the four different shapes—the cube, the sphere, the cylinder, and the cone—with one another. They may notice that the cone has a pointed end but the cylinder does not; that the cube has all flat sides and the sphere has none; and so on.

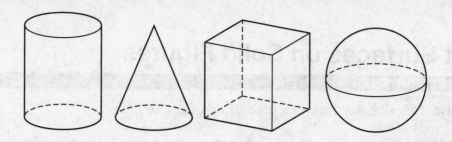

Comparing Solid Figures

ACCESS CONTENT; EXTEND LANGUAGE

Objective Identify solid figures that roll, stack, or slide on a flat surface.

Materials *(per group)* Geometric solids: sphere, cube, cylinder, cone

Vocabulary Roll, stack, slide

> **ESL Strategies** | ***Use before*** **LEARN** | 10–15 MIN

Use Gestures ➤ Hold up each geometric solid and name it. Invite children to repeat the names after you. **Now, let's find out which shapes <u>roll</u>, which shapes <u>stack</u>, and which shapes <u>slide</u>.** Make a rolling gesture with your hands, moving them forward. **I am rolling my hands.** Have children imitate your gesture. Then pantomine stacking your fists, one atop the other. **I am stacking my fists.** Have children imitate your action. Then slowly slide one hand across the desk. **I am sliding my hand across the desk.** Have children slide their hands across their desks. Repeat all three processes until the class can quickly match the three words—*roll, stack,* and *slide*—to their corresponding gestures.

Use Manipulatives ➤ Divide the class into groups. Have children in each group look at their solids. Hold up a sphere. **We want to see which shapes can roll. Can this shape roll? Why?** *(Yes, because it is round)* Invite the children in each group to roll the sphere from one child to another. **Do you see any other shapes that can roll?** Children should find that the cylinder rolls when it is placed on its curved or rounded side and that the cone rolls a little, but not in a straight line the way a can does.

Have Students Report Back Orally ➤ **Now find out which of your other shapes will stack and which will slide.** Have group members continue to experiment on their own with the four solid figures. (Allow two groups to work together to find out which of the four figures can be stacked.) Have volunteers report to the class about which shapes can roll, which shapes can stack, which shapes can slide—and why.

Flat Surfaces on Solid Figures

ACCESS CONTENT

Objective Describe the shape of a flat surface of a solid figure.

Materials *(per group)* Construction-paper plane shapes: circle, square, triangle; geometric solids: cube, cone, pyramid

Vocabulary Flat surface

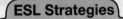 **ESL Strategies**   *Use before* **LEARN**   🕐 10–15 MIN

Use Demonstration ➤ Have children work in small groups. Give each group a set of construction-paper plane shapes and a set of geometric solids. (See Materials list above.) Show and name each shape and each solid. Then point to the four construction-paper shapes. **Do you see how these shapes are flat? They are called plane shapes because they are flat.** Discuss the word *plane* with children and tell them that *plane shapes* is a special math name for shapes that are flat.

Hold up each geometric solid (cube, cone, and pyramid) in turn. Have each group hold up the same shape as you say its name. Have children repeat the name with you. **These are called solid figures. Solid figures are not flat. Solid figures can have many sides or surfaces. Some of the sides are flat** (point to the six sides on the cube, as an example), **but the whole figure is not flat the way this square is** (hold up the construction-paper square as an example).

Use Small-Group Interactions ➤ Hold up the four construction-paper shapes. **We can match each of these plane shapes to the side of one of our solid figures. Each solid shape— except for the sphere—has one or more <u>flat surfaces</u>.** Have children repeat the term *flat surfaces* with you. Have them point out a few flat surfaces around the room. Then hold up the pyramid and point to one of its sides. **Look at the side of this pyramid. What shape is it?** Hold up the square plane shape against the pyramid. **Is the side of the pyramid this shape?** *(No)* Have children explain why not. Guide them to recognize that the triangle plane shape matches (is the same shape as) the side of the pyramid.

Divide the class into small groups. Have group members work together to identify the sides (or surfaces) of their 3 solid figures and match them with their 3 plane shapes. Encourage children to use math vocabulary to describe their plane shapes and solid figures. Have them informally explain to you how they matched plane shapes and flat surfaces.

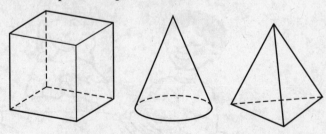

Squares and Other Rectangles

ACCESS CONTENT

Objective Identify and describe squares and other rectangles.

Materials Construction-paper squares and other rectangles in different sizes; book; paper napkin

Vocabulary Square, rectangle

ESL Strategies *Use before* **LEARN** 10 MIN

Use Demonstration ➤ Tell children that they will be learning more about <u>squares</u> and other <u>rectangles</u>. Give each child a square and a non-square rectangle and name the shapes as you pass them out. **Let's count the corners of our squares and our rectangles.** Explain that both have 4 corners, and both have 4 sides—but they have different shapes. **How does the rectangle look different from the square?** Lead children to look closely at the 4 sides of each shape. Explain that both shapes are called rectangles because they both have 4 corners and 4 sides. **But the square is a special kind of rectangle because its sides are all the same size. The rectangle has two short sides and two long sides.**

Use Real Objects ➤ Place two squares and two rectangles in the chalk tray. **Who can come up here and find the square rectangles?** If necessary, allow the volunteer to choose a friend to remind him or her what is special about the 4 sides of square rectangles. **All rectangles have 4 sides, but only square rectangles have 4 sides that match. How do they match? They are all the same length.** Have the child show the two square rectangles to the class. Point to the 4 equal sides. **Squares have 4 sides that are the same size, the same length.** Have the child show the two non-square rectangles to the class. Point to the 2 long sides and then to the 2 short sides. Guide children to see that they can recognize squares and other rectangles by their sides, but that the same shapes can come in different sizes. Draw a very large square on the board. Draw a very small square on the board. Draw a rectangle with 2 very long sides and 2 very short sides. Draw a rectangle with 2 long sides that are only a little bit longer than the short sides.

Use Pictures ➤ Display a square and a non-square rectangle in the chalk tray and have children name each shape. Then hold up a rectangular book. **What am I holding up?** *(A book)* **What shape is the side of this book?** *(Rectangle)* Have children discuss the shape of the book and the relative lengths of its parallel sides. Have them identify the book's shape using a complete sentence, as they are able: "The book is shaped like a rectangle." Hold up a paper napkin. **Which shape is this napkin?** *(A square)* Then ask all the children to look around the classroom and to point out other objects that are squares and non-square rectangles.

Circles and Triangles

ACCESS CONTENT

Objective Identify and describe circles and triangles.

Materials *(per pair)* Picture book that clearly shows objects shaped like circles and triangles; attribute blocks: circle and triangle

Vocabulary Circle, triangle

ESL Strategies *Use before* **LEARN** ⏱ 10–15 MIN

Use Pictures ➤ Begin by reading a book to children that clearly shows different-shaped objects. Then hold up <u>circle</u> and <u>triangle</u> attribute blocks. Have children repeat the names of the shapes with you. **These are shapes we see in our math book. They are also shapes we see every day. When we talked about this picture book, did you see any circles and triangles?**

Hold up an attribute-block circle. **What is this shape?** *(Circle)* **Is there something shaped like a circle in this picture in the book?** Trace the shape of the circle in the book with your finger and then the shape of the attribute block. **Let's look for something else that is shaped like a circle.** Continue looking for circles within the book's pictures, tracing shapes with your finger each time you find them. Invite children to help you find the circles. Hold up an attribute-block triangle. **Now let's look for a triangle in this book.** Continue in this manner until children have identified all or most of the triangles in the book.

Use ➤ Have children role-play reading picture books together, looking for circles
Peer Questioning and triangles in the pictures. Provide each pair with a circle and a triangle attribute block. Encourage children to ask and answer questions using sentences that include both the name of the shape (*circle* or *triangle*) and the name of the object in the picture.

Slides, Flips, and Turns

ACCESS CONTENT

Objective Identify a slide, a flip, and a turn.

Materials *(per child)* Large construction-paper rectangle, marked with a large dot in the upper, right-hand corner

Vocabulary Slide, flip, turn

ESL Strategies *Use before* **LEARN** ⏱ 10–15 MIN

Use Gestures ➤ Provide each child with a large rectangle and name the shape. Point out the dot in the upper, right-hand corner. Tell children they are going to learn that shapes can <u>slide</u>, <u>flip</u>, and <u>turn</u>. **I am holding a rectangle against the board. Now I am now going to slide it to my right. Did the rectangle change its** size or shape? *(No)* **What is different?** *(It moved; it changed its position.)* Emphasize that it is no longer in the same place but that it is still the same size and shape. Have children hold their shapes and practice sliding them with you. As you move, say the action aloud. Have children repeat the name of the action along with you.

Then tell children that they are going to see what happens when they flip their shapes. **Now I am going to flip this rectangle.** Demonstrate by flipping your rectangle all the way over so that the dot is no longer facing the children. **Did the rectangle change its size or shape?** *(No)* **What is different?** *(It moved. The dot is on the other side now.)* Have children pantomime flipping their rectangles with you as they say the name of the action. Repeat the process for turning, remembering to turn the shape on one of its points (corners), so that the shape ends up being on a diagonal.

Use ➤
Peer Questioning

Have pairs role-play the actions using their shapes. Encourage them to use a question-and-answer format as they talk about their shapes and the actions they are performing with them. For example: "Are you sliding your rectangle?" "Yes, I am sliding my rectangle." For children who are not ready to communicate in complete sentences, encourage them to name the action as they move the shape.

Combining and Separating Shapes

ACCESS CONTENT

USE WITH LESSON 8-7

Objective Recognize that shapes can be combined to make different shapes.

Materials *(per child)* Teacher-made page of shapes (made by tracing different combinations of attribute blocks; see below); 6 attribute blocks: 3 triangles, 3 squares

ESL Strategies **Use before** LEARN

⏱ 10 MIN

Use Manipulatives ➤ Distribute attribute blocks and a reproducible page showing the following shapes.

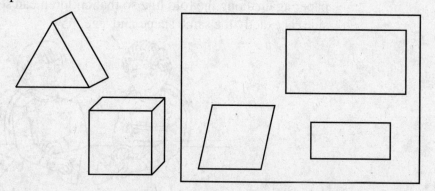

Provide each child with 3 triangle attribute blocks and 3 square attribute blocks. Hold up and name one square and one triangle. **You each have 3 squares. Each square is the same size. You each have 3 triangles. Each triangle is the same size. Now let's look at this page of different shapes.** Point to each shape and name it. Have children repeat the names of the shapes with you.

Explain to children that they can make new shapes using their attribute blocks. Point to the shapes on the reproducible page. **I'm going to start with this rhombus. How can I use my blocks to make it? I'm going to take one of my blocks—a triangle—and place it on top of this rhombus.** Tell children to watch you first and then to try it themselves.

Make sure that each child places the triangle as you have done. Then tell children that you are going to cover the rest of the shape. Model placing another triangle on the remaining half of the rhombus. **Do you see that the rhombus shape is covered?** *(Yes)* Slide the two triangle pieces to the side so that they are next to, instead of on top of, the rhombus. (See illustration below.) **Do the two shapes look the same?** *(Yes)* Repeat the process with children as you model making the two rectangles.

Symmetry

ACCESS CONTENT

Objective Identify shapes that are symmetrical.

Materials 1 piece of construction paper; marker; scissors; *(per pair)* envelope containing several construction-paper shapes cut in half to make 2 matching parts; tape

Vocabulary Matching parts

ESL Strategies

Use before **LEARN**

🕐 10–15 MIN

Use ➤ Demonstration

Display a piece of construction paper. **This is a whole piece of paper. Now watch as I fold it in half.** Mark the fold line with a marker. Have children describe the shape on each side of the fold line. Children may observe that the two parts are the same. **Yes, the two parts are the same. They are equal. They are halves. They are called <u>matching parts</u>. This fold line separates one matching part from the other matching part.** Fold the paper again along the fold line so that children can see that each part (each side) is exactly the same shape and size.

Cut along the fold line. Pass around each half for children to observe. Then put the two halves, the two matching parts, together again. **This is like a puzzle. We know that both pieces are matching parts because they are the same size and shape.**

Provide each pair of children with an envelope containing several construction-paper shapes cut in half to make two matching parts. Invite children to find the matching parts and tape them together. Have volunteers discuss their shapes and how they identified each shape's two matching parts.

Equal Parts

USE WITH LESSON 8-9

ACCESS CONTENT

Objective Identify equal parts of a whole.

Materials 3 apples; knife to cut apples; *(per pair)* partially peeled banana; paper plate; dull plastic knife

Vocabulary Whole, equal parts

ESL Strategies   *Use before*   **LEARN**   🕐 10–15 MIN

Use Real Objects ➤ Show children a whole apple. **This is a <u>whole</u> apple. It is whole because it has not been cut into parts.** Cut the apple into two unequal parts. Give each part of the apple to a different child. **Are your parts the same size?** *(No)* Then show another apple. **Is this a whole apple?** *(Yes)* **Now I am going to cut this apple into 2 <u>equal parts</u>. Are the parts the same size?** *(Yes)* Pass the two parts of the apple around so that everyone can see that the two parts are the same size. **This apple was cut into 2 parts that are the same size. They are called equal parts.**

Show a third whole apple and cut it into 2 equal parts. Then cut each of the halves again, making 4 equal parts. Follow the same procedure, questioning children as to whether the parts are the same size, or equal. **This apple has been cut into 4 parts. The parts are all the same size, so they are equal in size. This apple has been cut into 4 equal parts.**

Use Total ➤ Divide the class into pairs. Give each pair a partially peeled banana, a paper
Physical Response plate, and a dull plastic knife. Have children peel the rest of their bananas. **Do you have a whole banana?** *(Yes)* **Now try to cut your banana into 2 equal parts.** Circulate among pairs to make sure children are able to cut the bananas properly. Have a volunteer hold up the 2 halves of that pair's banana for the class to see. **Now cut your banana into 4 equal parts.** Have volunteers explain how they did this.

Halves and Fourths

EXTEND LANGUAGE

Objective Identify halves and fourths of a whole.

Materials 2 apples; knife to cut the apples

Vocabulary Halves, fourths

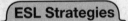 **ESL Strategies** *Use before* **LEARN**   ⏱ 10 MIN

Focus on Meaning ➤ Remind children that they have already learned about equal parts. Now they are going to learn about <u>halves</u> and <u>fourths</u>. Show children a whole apple. Cut the apple in half. **Are these parts the same size?** *(Yes)* **That's right. This apple has been cut into two equal parts. Both parts are the same size. Both parts are equal. When two parts are equal, they are called halves.**

Repeat the procedure again, but use apples drawn on the board to show halves. (See illustration below.) This will help children make the connection between three-dimensional and two-dimensional images.

Display another whole apple. Then cut it into fourths. **How many parts are there?** *(Four)* **Are they the same size or different sizes?** *(The same size)* **Are these parts halves?** *(No)* **Why not?** *(Halves are two equal parts, and that apple has been cut into four equal parts.)* **That's correct, and when four parts are equal, they are called fourths.** Have the class repeat the word *fourths* after you. Ask children if they hear a number word in the word *fourth*. Guide them to recognize the number word *four* in the word *fourths*. On the board, draw a picture of an apple cut into four equal parts to help children visualize *fourths*.

Problem-Solving Strategy:
Use Objects

ACTIVATE PRIOR KNOWLEDGE/BUILD BACKGROUND

Objective Solve problems involving equal shares.

Materials *(per pair)* "Worms" made out of short pieces of yarn

ESL Strategies *Use before* **LEARN**   ⏱ 10–15 MIN

Use Simulation ➤ Invite a group of three children to kneel beside you. Tell them that you are the mother bird, and they are baby birds in your nest. Have children explain what they know about birds and how birds feed their babies. Then show the class a handful of nine yarn pieces and explain that they are "worms." **Birds like to eat worms. Can you think of anything else that birds eat?** Pause and accept any reasonable responses. Then tell children that you want to feed your babies an equal amount of worms, and that this means that all 3 of your babies should get the same number of worms.

Model counting out the 9 "worms" starting with Baby Bird #1. Count 1 "worm" for Baby Bird #1; 1 "worm" for Baby Bird #2; 1 "worm" for Baby Bird #3, and so on. Repeat until each bird gets 3 worms. (And remind children that you are only pretending—that they are not to eat the yarn!) When you've finished counting, ask: **How many worms did each of my little baby birds get?** *(3)*

Repeat the process with another set of "baby birds" and a different, evenly divisible number of "worms."

Divide the class into pairs. Give each pair an even number of worms. Tell children that they need to share the worms equally. Have them role-play being birds as they divide their food and "eat" it up. Invite children to tell how many worms each bird ate and whether they each ate an equal share.

Problem-Solving Applications: I Spy

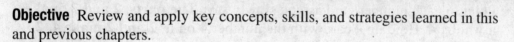

USE WITH LESSON 8-12

ACCESS CONTENT

Objective Review and apply key concepts, skills, and strategies learned in this and previous chapters.

Materials Geometric solids; shopping bag

ESL Strategies   *Use before* **LEARN**   🕐 10–15 MIN

Use Manipulatives ➤ Display the geometric solids and name each of them. Have the class repeat the name of each shape with you. Then pick up the cube and pass it around. **Tell me about this shape.** Help children notice that the cube has 8 corners and no rounded or curved surfaces. Count the corners together. Then pick up the pyramid. Again, have children describe the shape and count the number of corners. Continue this process for each of the remaining solids.

Use Total Physical Response ➤ Out of view of the children, place one of the solids in a bag. Invite a volunteer to reach into the bag, keeping his or her eyes closed. Have the child feel the solid, describe it, and name it. For instance, he or she might say, "It's round. It has no corners. It's a sphere." Then have the child pull the solid out of the bag to confirm the prediction. Repeat the process with additional volunteers and different solids.

It's round.
It has no
corners.
It's a sphere.

Ways to Make 4 and 5

USE WITH LESSON
9-1

ACCESS CONTENT

Objective Use counters to show 4 and 5 in two parts.

Materials Number Cards 0–11 (Teaching Tool 12)

Vocabulary Whole, part

ESL Strategies | **Use before** **LEARN** | 🕐 10–15 MIN

Use Total Physical Response ➤ Have 4 volunteers form two pairs. Point to the first pair. **How many children are in this group?** *(2)* Have one child in the first pair hold up a number 2 card. Repeat this process for the second group, with one child in the second group holding up a number 2 card as well. **There are 2 children in the first group and 2 children in the second group.** Move the two groups together. **How many children are there altogether?** *(4)* Point to each number card as you slowly say: **The <u>parts</u>, 2 and 2, make a <u>whole</u>, 4.** Hold up a card with the number 4 on it. **2 and 2 make 4. 2 and 2 is 4.**

Invite 4 other children to form two different-sized groups: one group of 1 and one group of 3. Repeat the process of counting children in each group and having a child in each group hold up the appropriate number card. **How many children are in each group, or each part?** *(1 and 3)* Move the groups together. **How many children are there altogether?** *(4)* Point to each group as you slowly say: **These two parts, 1 and 3, also make a whole of 4. 2 and 2 make 4. And 1 and 3 make 4. There are different parts that can make the same whole.** Ask children to paraphrase in their own words what you have just said. Repeat the process two more times with different groups of children forming whole groups of 5 children.

Ways to Make 6 and 7

ACTIVATE PRIOR KNOWLEDGE/BUILD BACKGROUND

Objective Show 6 and 7 in two parts.

Materials Clay; rolling pin; 2 different-shaped cookie cutters

Vocabulary Whole, part

ESL Strategies *Use before* **LEARN**   10–15 MIN

Connect to Prior
Experiences ➤

Roll out a ball of clay. Show the clay and two different-shaped cookie cutters to children and name them. **Today we will use cookie cutters and clay to help us look at groups of shapes.** Cut out 6 shapes from one cookie cutter and line them up. **How many (stars) are there?** *(6)* Point to each (star) as you count it aloud.

Use Gestures ➤

Use gestures as you say: **This whole group is made up of 6 (stars).** Cut out two (triangles) using the other cookie cutter and replace two of the (star) shapes with the new (triangle) shapes. **Now, one part of our whole group is (stars) and another part is (triangles).** Point to the (stars). **How many (stars) are there?** *(4)* Point to the (triangles). **How many (triangles) are there?** *(2)* **How many shapes are there altogether?** *(6)* **Yes, even though we traded 2 (stars) for 2 (triangles), we still have 6 shapes in the whole group.** Count each of the shapes aloud once again. Invite volunteers to tell about the <u>whole</u> and the <u>parts</u> in their own words. Encourage children to use complete sentences but allow them to answer nonverbally if necessary. Repeat the process, showing children another way to make a group of 6 using different numbers of the same two shapes. Then repeat the activity, making a whole of 7.

Ways to Make 8 and 9

ACCESS CONTENT

Objective Show 8 and 9 in two parts and in different ways.

Materials *(per group)* Ball of clay; rolling pin; 2 different-shaped cookie cutters

ESL Strategies

Use Total ➤
Physical Response

Use before **LEARN** 🕐 15–20 MIN

Divide the class into small groups. Distribute a ball of clay, a rolling pin, and 2 cookie cutters to each group. You may want to name the shapes as you pass them out. Have group members repeat the names of the shapes aloud.

Make 8 shapes with one of your cookie cutters and put them in a straight line. Make sure that each group correctly molds and cuts 8 shapes. **Is 8 the whole or the part?** *(The whole)* **Now make 2 different shapes with your other cookie cutter.** Ask children to replace the first two shapes in their line with the two new shapes they made. **How many shapes are in the first part of your group?** *(2)* **How many shapes are in the second part of your group?** *(6)*

Encourage small groups of children to describe their combinations to group members. For example: "2 stars and 6 squares are 8 shapes in all," or "2 and 6 make 8." Have children experiment with other combinations of 8. Encourage them to discuss their combinations within their group.

Then have children repeat the process, beginning with 9 uniform shapes.

Ways to Make 10

ACCESS CONTENT; EXTEND LANGUAGE

USE WITH LESSON
9-4

Objective Use a ten-frame to show 10 in different ways.

Materials *(per pair)* 10 two-color counters; Ten-Frame (Workmat 4); pink and yellow colored chalk

ESL Strategies

Use before **LEARN**

🕐 10–15 MIN

Use Demonstration ➤ On the board, draw a ten-frame. To the side of the frame, draw the outlines of 10 counters. Have children work in pairs. Pass out 10 two-color counters and a ten-frame to each pair. **I gave each pair of you ten counters.** Have children count their counters aloud with you. **I've drawn my 10 counters and my ten-frame on the board. I want to fill the ten-frame with 10 counters, but I want some to be red-side-up, and some to be yellow-side-up.** Use the colored chalk to fill half of the ten-frame with "counters" that are yellow-side-up. **Let's count how many yellow-side-up counters I've just put in the frame. "1, 2, 3, 4, 5." How many red-side-up counters do I need to fill in the rest of the frame?** Have children count aloud with you as you draw red-side-up counters one by one: **"1. 2. 3. 4. 5." How many counters do I have in all?** *(10)* Have children count aloud with you again. **I made 2 sets of 5 counters. That's how I made 10.** Repeat the activity, drawing 8 yellow-sided counters first. **If I put 8 yellow-side-up counters in the frame, how many red-side-up counters do I need to fill all 10 boxes in the frame?** Make sure children understand you need 2.

Have pairs work to fill their ten-frames with the same combination of counters as you just drew on the board. Repeat, using another variation, modeling on the board and having children copy with their counters. **Each time you fill the ten-frame, you can do a different combination of counters. But what's always going to be the same if you fill every box in the frame?** *(There will be 10 counters in all.)*

Have Students Report Back Orally ➤ Have pairs invent their own combinations of yellow- and red-side-up counters to fill up their ten-frames. Then have them report to the class on how many of each counter they used to fill their ten-frame. Write their combinations on the board, such as: "4 yellow-side-up counters + 6 red-side-up counters." Check with children to make sure the combinations make 10 in all.

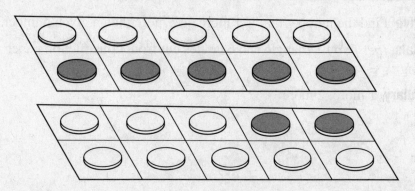

Problem-Solving Strategy: Make an Organized List

USE WITH LESSON 9-5

ACCESS CONTENT

Objective Solve problems by making an organized list showing two parts of 5 to 10 items.

Materials 5 two-color counters; Ten-Frame (Workmat 4); *(per pair)* 10 two-color counters; Ten-Frame (Workmat 4); lined paper

ESL Strategies *Use before* **LEARN** 🕐 15–20 MIN

> **Use Graphic Organizers**

Tell children that they are going to learn all of the ways to make 5. Draw a two-column chart on the board. Display a ten-frame. Fill the top row of the frame with five red counters. **How many red counters are there?** *(5)* **How many yellow counters are there?** *(0)* Tell children that you are going to write the number of red counters in the first column, and the number of yellow counters in the second column. Then point to the numbers as you say: **5 red counters and 0 yellow counters make 5 counters in all.** Have children repeat the sentence after you, as they are able.

We know that 5 and 0 make 5. Now let's figure out all of the other ways that we can make 5. Turn over one of the red counters. **Now how many red counters are there?** *(4)* **How many yellow counters are there?** *(1)* Write this new combination of 5 on the board. Tell children to repeat after you: **4 red and 1 yellow makes 5.** Continue in this manner as you make all of the other combinations of 5 (3 and 2, 2 and 3, 1 and 4, and 0 and 5).

> **Use Small-Group Interactions**

Divide the class into pairs. Give each pair 10 two-color counters, a ten-frame, and a sheet of lined paper. Instruct each pair to fold their paper lengthwise, so that they can make a two-column chart. Then have children trace along the fold line. Have all children begin by filling their entire ten-frame with same-colored counters (e.g., all red). Then have pairs work together to make all of the combinations of 10 and record their findings on their charts. After children have completed their charts, invite volunteers to read each of the "sentences" for 10 (e.g., "7 red and 3 yellow make 10").

1 More and 2 More

USE WITH LESSON 9-6

ACTIVATE PRIOR KNOWLEDGE/BUILD BACKGROUND

Objective Find the number that is 1 more or 2 more than a given number.

Materials *(per pair)* 1 triangle and 6 circles cut from construction paper; masking tape

Vocabulary 1 more, 2 more

ESL Strategies *Use before* **LEARN**

Connect to Prior ➤ Ask children to raise their hands if they like ice cream. Ask children to name
Experiences   their favorite flavors. Ask them if they have ever bought an ice cream cone
from an ice cream vendor, or salesperson. If so, ask volunteers to describe
what happened. **Guess what! I am selling ice cream today! Who would
like to come up here and buy some? Here is one scoop of ice cream,
(Child).** On the board, tape your construction-paper cone (triangle) and one
scoop (circle) to the board. (And have the child pretend to give you some
money for his or her purchase.) **Do you want <u>1 more</u> scoop, (Child)?** *(Yes)*
Tape another "scoop" on the board (and again role-play an exchange of
money for the purchase). **How many are 1 and 1 more?** *(2)* Have children
count the scoops aloud. Then have children repeat, as they are able, "1 scoop
and 1 more scoop makes 2 scoops." Repeat the activity a few times, using a
different number of scoops in each initial group.

Invite another volunteer to "buy" an ice cream cone from you. **Here are 2
scoops of ice cream. Do you want <u>2 more</u>?** *(Yes)* Add two more scoops to
the cone on the board. **How many are 2 and 2 more?** *(4)* **That's right, 2
and 2 more are 4.** Have children repeat the sentence "2 and 2 more are 4"
after you, as they are able.

Use Role Playing ➤ Divide the class into pairs. Give each pair several scoops of "ice cream" and
a construction-paper cone. Have pairs take turns role-playing selling ice
cream and adding scoops to the cone. Encourage children to explain in
sentences or words what has happened each time another scoop has been
added. For instance, "3 scoops and 1 more scoop are 4 scoops."

1 Fewer and 2 Fewer

USE WITH LESSON **9-7**

ACCESS CONTENT/EXTEND LANGUAGE

Objective Find the number that is 1 fewer or 2 fewer than a given number.

Materials 5 construction-paper kites; 6 classroom toys

Vocabulary 1 fewer, 2 fewer

ESL Strategies *Use before* **LEARN**   10 MIN

Use Total ➤ Have 4 children stand. **How many children are standing?** *(4)* Tell 1 child to
Physical Response   sit down. Point to the group still standing. **Now how many children are
standing?** *(3)* **There were 4 children standing. Then one child sat down. 3
children are how many fewer than 4 children?** *(1 fewer)* Count the
number of children standing aloud. Encourage children to say, in unison with
you, as they are able, "3 children are 1 fewer than 4 children."

Use Gestures ➤ Repeat the activity, using a different number of items. For instance, tape 5
construction-paper kites to the board and count them aloud. Then gesture broadly
as you show 2 of the kites flying away. **Uh-oh! 2 of our kites are flying away!**

Count the remaining kites with children. **There were 5 kites, and then 2 of them flew away. 3 kites are how many fewer than 5 kites?** (*2 fewer*) Have children repeat, as they are able, "3 kites are 2 fewer than 5 kites."

Display 6 classroom toys on a table. Ask a child to put 2 toys back where they belong. **There were 6 toys in all. Then (Child) put 2 of them away. 4 toys are how many fewer than 6 toys?** (*2 fewer*) Have children repeat after you, as they are able, "4 toys are 2 fewer than 6 toys."

Have Children ➤ Report Back Orally

Display 5 toys and ask a child to put 1 of them away. Have another child use complete sentences to explain what happened. For example: "There were 5 toys. Then (Child) put 1 away. There are 4 toys left. 4 toys are 1 fewer than 5 toys." Continue in the same manner, using other small quantities of toys.

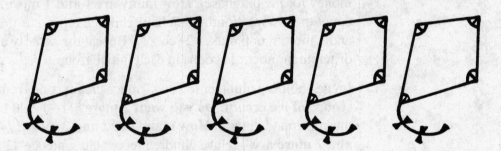

Problem-Solving Applications: Visit, Look, and Learn

USE WITH LESSON 9-8

ACCESS CONTENT

Objective Review and apply key concepts, skills, and strategies learned in this and previous chapters.

Materials (*per pair*) Number Cards 0–11 (Teaching Tool 12); 2–6 cut-out shapes (big and small); construction paper; glue; 2 whole sheets and 4 half-sheets of construction paper

ESL Strategies

Use before **LEARN**   🕐 10–15 MIN

Use ➤ Demonstration

Tape 2 whole sheets and 4 half-sheets of construction paper onto the board. Tell children that they are rectangles. Then count the number of rectangles aloud. Say: **There are 6 rectangles. Let's count the number of big rectangles.** Have a volunteer point to the shapes that are big, and count them aloud. Write the number 2 on the board. **Now let's count the number of small rectangles.** Have another volunteer point to them and count them aloud. Write the number 4 on the board. Point to the 2 and the 4 and say: **There are 2 big rectangles and 4 small rectangles. How many rectangles are there altogether?** (*6*)

Use Small-Group ➤
Interactions

Then tape 2 big rectangles on the board. Say: **There are 2 big rectangles in this group: 1, 2. If there are 5 rectangles altogether** (sweep your hands) **how many small rectangles are there?** *(3)* Invite a volunteer to tape three small rectangles to the board. Repeat this process several times for numbers under 6.

Provide pairs with a number card between 2–6 and an accompanying number of big and small cut-out shapes. Tell children to use any combination of shapes to make the number on their number card. Have them glue the shapes onto a piece of construction paper and write the number of big and small shapes. Tell them to circle the number that is more.

Stories About Joining

USE WITH LESSON 10-1

ACTIVATE PRIOR KNOWLEDGE/BUILD BACKGROUND

Objective Act out number stories that involve joining two groups.

Materials 4 bowls

Vocabulary Number story, join, in all

ESL Strategies

Use before **LEARN**

⏱ 10–15 MIN

Connect to Prior Experiences ➢ Have children talk about any pets they may have. Ask how many of them have dogs. Count the number of raised hands and write that number on the board. Ask how many have cats; write that number on the board. Then ask children to identify whether more children have dogs or cats.

Invite four children to the front of the class. Assign two children to be "dogs" and two children to be "cats." Tell children that you are going to tell them a number story. Explain that a number story is a story in which the numbers are very important. Gesture toward the dogs. **How many dogs are there?** *(2)* Gesture toward the cats. **How many cats are there?** *(2)* Write "2 and 2" on the board. **Uh-oh! Our pets are hungry. It's dinnertime!** Call on another child to set four bowls on the floor between the two groups of pets. Then have the two groups join together and role-play eating their food from the four bowls. **Look! We joined the groups together. How many pets are there in all?** *(4)*

Complete the sentence on the board so that it reads "2 and 2 is 4." Have children read the number story with you as you point to each part. Repeat the activity, telling other number stories about four things, and using different combinations.

Use Role Playing ➢ Divide the class into groups of four. Tell children to think of a story about the number 4. Then have them role-play the story. You may want to provide a couple of examples to stir their thinking: **2 children could be lions, and 2 children could be elephants. Or 3 children could be elephants, and 1 child could be a chicken.** Have children form two separate groups and then join their groups.

Joining Groups

ACCESS CONTENT

Objective Interpret illustrations that show joining groups and write the corresponding numbers.

Materials 2 toy cars; 4 toy trucks; *(per pair)* 6 blocks

Vocabulary Altogether

ESL Strategies

Use before **LEARN**

 10–15 MIN

Use Real Objects ➤ Hold up a toy car and a toy truck and name them. Explain to children that they are going to join two groups together. Place two cars on a desk. **How many cars are there in this group?** *(2)* Place four trucks on the desk. **How many trucks are there in this group?** *(4)* Explain to children that there are two groups: one group has 2 cars, and one group has 4 trucks.

Push the 2 cars and the 4 trucks together to create a single group. **I had one group that had 2 cars in it. And I had another group that had 4 trucks in it. Then I joined the two groups together. That means that I made one group out of the two groups. How many groups do I have?** *(1)* **And how many toys are there altogether in my new group?** *(6)* On the board write "2 and 4 is 6." Read the sentence as you point to each part.

Paraphrase Ideas ➤ Have volunteers explain in their own words what happened when you joined the two groups. Repeat this activity, using different items, and using a different number of items in each group.

Divide the class into pairs and give each pair 6 blocks. Write the following sentence frame on the board: "_____ and _____ is _____." Have each pair make two groups with their blocks and then join the groups together. Have children write a sentence that explains their grouping, for example, "3 and 3 is 6." Then have each child explain to his or her partner what the number sentence means.

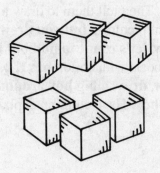

Problem-Solving Strategy: Draw a Picture

ACCESS CONTENT

Objective Solve problems by drawing pictures about joining two groups.

Materials *(per pair)* 5 foam "worms" (such as those used for packing and shipping); 5 toothpicks; small tub of water; drawing paper; crayons

ESL Strategies   *Use before* **LEARN**   🕐 15–20 MIN

Use Real Objects ➤ Divide the class into pairs and give each pair 5 "worms," 5 toothpicks, and a small tub of water. Have children insert a toothpick into each worm to transform it into a "boat."

Write "2 and 3 is 5" on the board and read it aloud. Then have children place 2 boats in the water and 3 boats out of the water. **Let's pretend that the boats in the water are fishing boats. How many fishing boats are there?** *(2)* **And let's pretend that the boats out of the water are sailboats. How many sailboats are there?** *(3)* Have children place the 3 "sailboats" in the water. **Now how many boats are in the water altogether?** *(5)*

Paraphrase Ideas ➤ Ask children to draw a picture of their 2 fishing boats and to write a 2 below the picture. Then tell them to draw a picture of their 3 sailboats and to write a 3 below that picture. **First you drew 2 boats. Then you added 3 more boats. Now, let's count to find out how many boats there are altogether.** Count the boats with children: **"1, 2, 3, 4, 5." Yes, 2 boats and 3 boats are 5 boats. Now, draw a big box around all 5 of your boats. Then write a 5 under the box.** Have children explain in their own words what they did.

Using the Plus Sign

ACCESS CONTENT

Objective Use the plus sign (+) to represent joining groups when recording addition.

Materials Number Cards 0–11 (Teaching Tool 12); plus-sign (+) card
(Teaching Tool 22); 3 red squares; 2 blue squares; masking tape

Vocabulary Add, plus sign

ESL Strategies

Use Total ➤
Physical Response

Use before **LEARN**

🕐 10–15 MIN

Tell children that they will learn about the word <u>add</u>. Tape 3 red squares and 2 blue squares next to each other on the board. **How many red squares are there?** *(3)* **How many blue squares are there?** *(2)* Write 3 under the group of red squares and 2 under the group of blue squares. Then move the two groups of squares together. **We can join, or add, the red squares and the blue squares.** Draw a ring around all 5 shapes. **How many squares are there in all?** *(5)* Count the shapes aloud and write 5 below the ring.

Make 2 large circles on the floor with masking tape. Have 2 children stand inside one of the circles. **How many children are in this circle?** *(2)* Place the number card for 2 near the circle. Have 3 children stand inside the other circle. **How many children are in this circle?** *(3)* Place the number card for 3 near the second circle. Then show children the symbol for +. **This is called a <u>plus sign</u>. You use it when you join, or add, two groups together.** Put the + sign between the number cards for 2 and 3 and, using gestures, say: **2 plus 3.** Then have the 2 children in the first group join the 3 children in the second group. Count together all the children inside the second circle. **How many children are there in all in our new group?** *(5)* Place the number card for 5 near the other two numbers. Read the sentence as children repeat after you: **"2 plus 3 is 5."**

Repeat the activity several times, using different combinations to make 6.

Finding the Sum

ACCESS CONTENT

Objective Identify and use the equal sign (=); add and write the sum.

Materials 2 bags; Number Cards 0–11 (Teaching Tool 12); 10 two-color counters; plus-sign (+) card and equal-sign (=) card (Teaching Tool 22); *(per pair)* 2 boxes; 2 two-color counters; 2 different-colored sheets of construction paper

Vocabulary Equal sign, sum, add

ESL Strategies   *Use before* **LEARN**   10–15 MIN

Use ➤
Demonstration

In advance, gather 2 bags, 2 sets of number cards 1–5, a plus-sign (+) card, an equal-sign (=) card, and a box of 10 two-color counters. Place one set of number cards in each bag. Ask two children to come forward. Have each child select a number card from a bag and place the card and the matching number of counters on a table. **(Child A) put down (3) counters. (Child B) put down (2) counters.** Place the plus-sign (+) card between the two number cards. **We can find out how many counters there are in all by joining the counters together. When you join two groups, you <u>add</u> them together. How many counters are there in all?** Place the number card for (5) on the table near the (3) and the (2). Then place the equal-sign (=) card between the second addend and the sum. Point to the <u>equal sign</u>. **This is called an equal sign. It means "equals" or "is the same as." (3) + (2) equals (5). (3) + (2) is the same as (5).** Point to the number card for 5. **This is called the <u>sum</u>. The sum tells how many there are in all.** Continue with sums to 7.

Use Manipulatives ➤

Give each pair of children 2 boxes, 7 two-color counters, and 2 different colors of construction paper. Write the number 1 on the board. **Put 1 counter in one box. Put the other counters in the other box.** Then have children empty each box and count the counters. **How many counters were in the first box?** *(1)* **How many counters were in the other box?** *(6)* Write 1 + 6 on the board. **How many counters are there in all?** *(7)* Complete the equation by writing = 7. Repeat the activity with all of the other combinations with sums of 7.

Addition Sentences

ACCESS CONTENT

Objective Write and solve addition sentences to represent joining situations.

Materials 6 large, blue construction-paper circles; tape

Vocabulary Addition sentence, equal sign

ESL Strategies   *Use before* **LEARN**   10 MIN

Use ➤
Demonstration

Display 6 large, blue construction-paper circles. **How many circles are there in all?** *(6)* Write the number 6 on the board and draw two columns below it. Divide the circles into groups of 4 and 2 and tape the groups in the columns. (See illustration.)

Pointing to the first column, ask: **How many circles are in this group?** *(4)* Pointing to the second column, ask: **How many circles in this group?** *(2)* Write 4 and 2 beneath the columns and then sweep your hand across all of the circles and ask: **How many circles are there in all?** *(6)* **Yes, there are 6 circles in all. 6 is the sum. The sum tells how many there are in all. And this is how we write the <u>addition sentence</u> that tells what we just did.** Write $4 + 2 = 6$ on the board. Read the sentence aloud as you point to each part. Then point to the equal sign and explain: **Remember, this is called an <u>equal sign</u>. It usually comes just before the sum.** Repeat for other sums of 6.

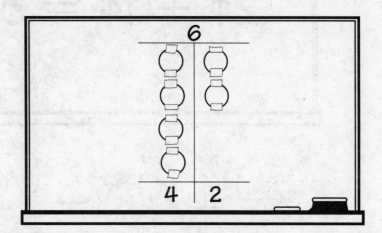

Adding Pennies

ACCESS CONTENT

USE WITH LESSON 10-7

Objective Add pennies, write addition sentences, and use the ¢ sign.

Materials *(per group)* Small cup of pennies

ESL Strategies   ***Use before***   **LEARN**   ⏱ 10 MIN

Use Demonstration ➤ Write a simple addition problem, such as $2 + 1 = $ _____, horizontally on the board. **Let's solve this problem together.** Have children read the math sentence aloud, filling in the blank with the correct answer. Then write the answer on the board and read the number sentence: **$2 + 1 = 3$.**

Use Real Objects ➤ **Now let's see how this problem would look if we were adding pennies.** Write a cent sign on the board and explain that the cent symbol is used to show pennies. Display a penny and name it. Then point to the cent symbol and name it. **Now I'm going to show you how we use the cent symbol in math problems.** Write the same math problem as before, but this time incorporate the cent symbols into the equation. Then read the sentence aloud. **This math problem says, "2 cents plus one cent equals 3 cents."**

Once again, hold up a penny and ask: **What is this?** *(A penny)* Then point to a cent sign and ask: **What is this?** *(A cent sign)* **Now let's find the problems that have pennies in them.** Write several math problems on the board. Have volunteers point to the problems that have pennies in them.

Circle the two money problems and have the class read them aloud. Then have children show on their desks what the first circled sentence looks like, using their pennies.

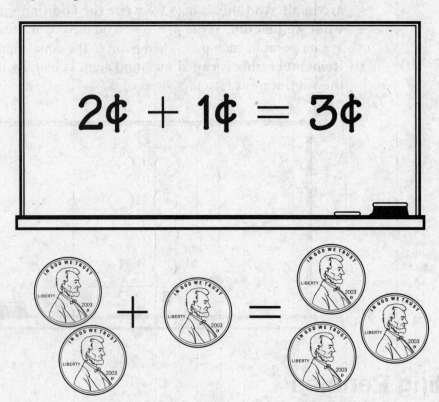

Problem-Solving Applications: Look Alikes

USE WITH LESSON

10-8

ACCESS CONTENT

Objective Review and apply key concepts, skills, and strategies learned in this and previous chapters.

Materials Pictures cut from magazines of fruits, vegetables, meats, and other food groups; *(per pair)* small classroom objects for sorting, such as cars and trucks, marbles and balls, pencils and crayons

ESL Strategies   ***Use before*** **LEARN**   🕐 15–20 MIN

Use Pictures ➤ From magazines, cut pictures of groups of food items, such as fruits, vegetables, and meats. Talk about the various foods and name them. Tell children the category that each food belongs to, for example: **This is a banana. It is a fruit.** After you have done this several times, encourage children to name the category of the food as you hold up each picture.

Model sorting the pictures in various ways, such as by color, size, and shape. Then sort the foods by type, such as fruits and vegetables. **The foods are sorted into 2 groups. Who can name the groups?** *(Fruits and vegetables)* **That's right. Let's count how many different pieces of (or kinds of) fruit there are.** Count the number of fruits aloud as children count with you. Write 3 on the board. **Now let's count the vegetables.** Count the vegetables aloud and write + 2 on the board. Read the addition problem on the board and discuss with children how to solve it. Then sort the foods another way and repeat the process.

Use Real Objects ➤ Have children work in pairs. Give each pair several different types of classroom objects, such as cars and trucks, marbles and balls, or pencils and crayons. Invite children to find different ways to sort the objects. Then have them write an addition sentence to illustrate how the items were sorted into two groups and how the two groups were then combined.

Separating

USE WITH LESSON 11-1

ACTIVATE PRIOR KNOWLEDGE/BUILD BACKGROUND; EXTEND LANGUAGE

Objective Act out number stories that involve separating two groups.

Materials 4 apples or construction-paper apple cutouts; shopping bag

Vocabulary Left

ESL Strategies   *Use before* **LEARN**   ⏱ 10–15 MIN

Use Role Playing ➤ Choose two volunteers to help you act out a shopping situation. Give "Bob" a shopping bag as he role-plays shopping for apples. Have "Ray" wait for "Bob" outside of the "store."

Display 4 apples or apple cutouts as you tell children the following number story: **Bob buys 4 apples.** (Have "Bob" put 4 apples in his shopping bag.) **He gives 2 of the apples to his friend Ray.** (Have "Bob" take two apples out of the bag and give them to "Ray.") **How many apples does Bob have <u>left</u> in his bag?** (Have "Bob" take the remaining apples out of his bag and count them aloud: "1 apple, 2 apples.") **Bob has 2 apples left.**

Focus on Meaning ➤ Tell children that the word *left* has more than one meaning. **Raise your left hand.** Check to make sure that all children are raising the correct hand. *Left can mean a direction, for example, when someone says, "turn left at the stop sign." Left c*an also mean "still here." If I ask you, "How many apples are left?" that is another way of asking you, "How many apples are still here?"** Have children offer examples of simple phrases or sentences that include the word *left*.

1 apple, 2 apples
Here are 2 apples.

Take Away

USE WITH LESSON 11-2

ACCESS CONTENT

Objective Determine how many are left when some objects in a group are taken away.

Materials 6 small toys, such as marbles, tops, dolls, or cars

Vocabulary Take away

ESL Strategies

Use Real Objects ➤

Use before LEARN

10–15 MIN

Show children 6 small toys and name them. Have children count the toys with you. **I have a group of 6 toys. Now I'm going to choose 2 of the toys to play with. I will <u>take away</u> 2 toys from this group of 6 toys.** Use gestures to demonstrate the action of "taking away" as you choose 2 of the toys and move them to your desk. Then write "6 take away 2 is ___ " on the board and read it aloud, saying "how many" when you point to the question mark. **How many toys are left?** Count the number of toys left on the table. Then return to the board, erase the question mark, and replace it with the number 4.

Count the number of toys remaining: **1, 2, 3, 4 toys. Now I have 4 toys left in this group.** Invite a volunteer to take away 1 of the 4 toys and take it back to his or her table. **(Child) took away 1 toy. Now how many toys are left in this group?** Write "4 take away 1 is ___ " on the board and read it aloud. Have a volunteer count the remaining number of toys and fill in the blank on the board. Then have a volunteer read the number story on the board as you point to each part: "4 take away 1 is 3." Repeat this procedure until there are no toys remaining. Each time, have a volunteer describe how many toys are left.

Comparing

ACCESS CONTENT

USE WITH LESSON 11-3

Objective Compare two groups to find out how many more or fewer.

Vocabulary More, fewer

ESL Strategies

Use ➤
Demonstration

Use before LEARN

10 MIN

On the board, draw 3 small, filled-in circles. Next to (but apart from) the circles, draw 4 squares. **I want to find out whether there are <u>more</u> dots or more squares.** Tell children that they will first need to look at what they are comparing. Then have children count the dots and squares aloud with you. **There are 3 dots and 4 squares. Which group has more, the group of dots or the group of squares?** *(The group of squares)* **Why?** *(Because 4 is more than 3)* **Let's check to see just how much more 4 is.** Draw a line from each dot to each square. Hold up 1 finger as you say: **I have 1 square left. So there is 1 more square than there are dots.** Write "1 more" on the board. Repeat the activity with different numbers of shapes to show the meaning of <u>fewer</u>.

Use Pantomime ➤ Review with children the steps you took to find out that there was 1 more square than there were dots. Allow ample time for children to fill in the blank as you pantomime the necessary response. **First we . . .** (pantomime looking) **at the two groups. That's right, first we looked at the two groups. Then we . . .** (pantomime counting). **Yes, then we counted each dot and each square. Then we . . .** (pantomime drawing matching lines). **Yes, then we matched the dots to the squares.** Use gestures and rhythm as you repeat the following summation two or three times: **We looked, we counted, we matched.** Invite children to repeat the summation along with you, as they make the corresponding gestures.

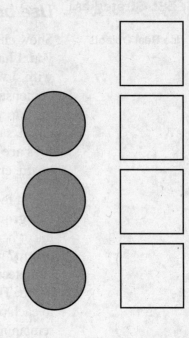

Using the Minus Sign

ACCESS CONTENT

USE WITH LESSON 11-4

Objective Use the minus sign (−) to represent "take away" situations when recording subtraction.

Materials *(per pair)* 5 connecting cubes; Number Cards 0–11 (Teaching Tool 12)

Vocabulary Minus sign, subtract

ESL Strategies *Use before* **LEARN**   🕐 10–15 MIN

Use Demonstration ➤ Tell children that they will learn about the word <u>subtract</u>. Display a stack of 5 blocks on a table and count them with children. **How many blocks are there in all?** *(5)* Write 5 on the board. Then have a child remove 1 block. **How many blocks did (Child) take away?** *(1)* Write 1 on the board below the 5. Then write a minus sign to the left of the 1. Point to it and tell children that it is called a <u>minus sign</u>. **A minus sign is used when we take away, or subtract, one number from another number.** Explain to children that you just subtracted, or took away, 1 block from the 5 blocks. Count the remaining blocks with children. **How many blocks are left?** *(4)* Draw a line under the 1 and write 4 below the 1. Read the subtraction fact aloud and have children repeat it after you. Then repeat the process, subtracting other numbers from 5.

Use Small-Group Interactions ➤ Give each pair of children number cards for 1–5 and a stack of 5 connecting cubes. Model counting the cubes in the stack. **There are 5 cubes in this tower.** Place the number card for 5 in the chalk tray. Remove 2 cubes as you say: **I am taking away 2 cubes.** Point to the remaining cubes and count them. **There are 3 cubes left.** Place the number card for 3 in the chalk tray.

Have children use the connecting cubes and number cards to practice taking away different numbers of cubes from 5. Have them talk about the subtraction process as they are working.

Finding the Difference

ACCESS CONTENT

USE WITH LESSON 11-5

Objective Use the equal sign (=); subtract and write the difference.

Materials 5 construction-paper circles; 1 bag; teacher-made subtraction fact cards to 6; 6 toy cars

Vocabulary Equal sign, subtract, difference

ESL Strategies

Use before LEARN

🕐 10–15 MIN

Use ➢
Demonstration

Tape five construction-paper circles vertically to the board. Count them with children and write 5 under them. Have a child take away, or subtract, 3 of the circles. To the right of the 5 write − 3. **This says 5 minus 3. What is 5 minus, or take away, 3?** *(2)* Have children count the number of construction-paper circles that are left. **There are 2 circles left. When you subtract, the part that is left is called the difference. This time, 2 is the difference.** Complete the number sentence by writing = 2 after the 3. Point to the equal sign and name it. **This is called an equal sign. Now our number sentence says 5 minus 3 equals 2. That means that 5 minus 3 is the same as 2. 5 minus 3 is 2. They are two names for the same amount.**

Make cards showing subtraction problems (facts to 6, such as 6 − 4) and place them in a bag. Display 6 toy cars on a table. Draw a card from the bag and display it. Read it aloud, saying, for example: **6 minus 4.** Group 6 toy cars together. Count them aloud. Point to the number 6 on the card and say: **We have 6 cars. The card says "6 minus 4."** Write 6 − 4 on the board. "Drive" 4 cars across the table and "park" them in a different spot. Have children say "**6 minus 4**" with you. **How many cars are left?** *(2)* Write = 2 on the board after the 4 and read the number sentence: **6 − 4 = 2.** Circle the 2 and say: **2 is the difference. The difference tells how many are left.** Have children repeat the activity, each time identifying the difference.

Subtraction Sentences

ACCESS CONTENT; ACTIVATE PRIOR KNOWLEDGE/BUILD BACKGROUND

Objective Write and solve subtraction sentences to represent take-away situations.

Materials 5 construction-paper "crackers"; 4 books

Vocabulary Subtraction sentence, equal sign

ESL Strategies   *Use before* **LEARN**   🕐 10–15 MIN

Use Total Physical Response ➤ Have 6 volunteers stand in front of the class. **How many children are standing up here?** *(6)* Tell 2 children to sit down. Point to the group still standing. **How many children are in the standing-up group now?** *(4)* **There were 6 children standing up. Then 2 children sat down. 4 children are left standing up.** Write $6 - 2 = 4$ horizontally on the board and read the sentence with children. Point to the sentence and explain that it is called a <u>subtraction sentence</u>. **A subtraction sentence has a minus sign and an <u>equal sign</u>.** Have volunteers point to and identify the minus sign and the equal sign. Explain to children that the equal sign means that $6 - 2$ on one side is the same as 4 on the other side. **$6 - 2$ is a way to make 4. $6 - 2$ and 4 are two names for the same amount.** Repeat the activity, using other subtraction facts.

Use Role Playing ➤ Tape 5 "crackers" to the board and count them with children. Tell children that you have a hungry little mouse in your hand. Then remove 2 crackers from the board and pretend to feed them to the mouse. Count the remaining crackers with children. **How many crackers are left?** *(3)* Using gestures, say: **There were 5 crackers. Then the little mouse ate 2 of them. 3 crackers are left.** Write $5 - 2 = 3$ on the board. **This is the subtraction sentence that tells about the little number story I just told you.**

Display 4 books on a table. Ask a child to put 3 books back on the bookshelf. **There were 4 books. Then (Child) put 3 of them away. How many books are left?** *(1)* Then write the appropriate subtraction sentence horizontally on the board: $4 - 3 = 1$. Have children identify the equal sign. Repeat the process, using other small quantities of books.

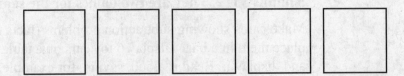

Subtracting Pennies

ACCESS CONTENT; EXTEND LANGUAGE

Objective Subtract pennies, write subtraction sentences, and use the ¢ sign.

Materials *(per child)* 10 pennies; *(per group)* cup; toys with price labels up to 10 cents each

---

ESL Strategies

Use before **LEARN**

🕐 10–15 MIN

Use Real Objects ➤ Divide the class into small groups. At each group's table, have a cup and various items labeled with prices, none higher than 10 cents. Tell children that today they will each "buy" one of the things on their table. Explain that you will buy something too. Give each child 10 pennies. **How many pennies is 10 cents?** *(10 pennies)* Write 10¢ on the board. Emphasize the cent sign. Then have children count their pennies and give you a "thumbs up" when they have counted 10 cents.

I have 10 cents, too. Model buying a toy for 4 cents. Count off each penny as you drop it into the cup: **1 cent, 2 cents, 3 cents, 4 cents. Now how many cents do I have left?** *(6¢)* Count each of the 6 remaining pennies aloud with children.

Write 10¢ − 4¢ = 6¢ on the board. As you write the sentence, say: **I started with 10 cents. I bought a (dinosaur) for 4 cents. I took away the 4 cents and put them in the cup. What is another way to say "take away"?** *(Minus)* **So 10 cents minus 4 cents is 6 cents.** Have children repeat that last sentence along with you, as they are able.

Have Students ➤ Have group members each "buy" something from the collection at their
Report Back table. Have children take turns and count out the pennies they are spending
Orally and the pennies they have left as they shop. (You can encourage those who aren't shopping to count along with the shopper.) As you visit each group, encourage children to describe what they are doing as they make their purchases. Have children who are ready to do so write number sentences to describe their transactions.

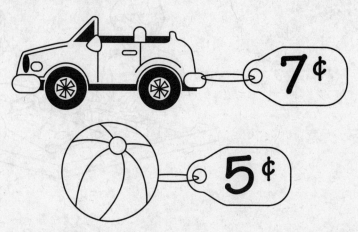

Problem-Solving Skill: Choose an Operation

ACCESS CONTENT; EXTEND LANGUAGE

Objective Solve problems by choosing addition or subtraction.

Materials 7 pencils; 5 books; 10 color tiles; *(per pair)* 10 color tiles; index card with an addition or subtraction sentence written on it

ESL Strategies

Use before LEARN

🕐 10–15 MIN

Use **>**
Demonstration

Display 4 pencils. Count each pencil as you place it on a table. **How many pencils are there?** *(4)* **Now I am going to put down 3 more pencils. How many pencils are there now?** *(7)* **Did I join two groups of pencils together, or did I take away one group from another group?** *(You joined two groups.)* **Did I add or subtract?** *(You added.)* Write $4 + 3 = 7$ on the board. Have a volunteer read the number sentence aloud as you point to each part.

Display 5 books. Count each book aloud. **How many books are there?** *(5)* Take away 3 books. **I took away 3 books. Who can tell me another word for "take away"?** *(Minus)* **We can also say 5 minus 3.** Write $5 - 3$ on the board and say: **Now, how many books are left?** *(2)* Continue with other number stories, both addition and subtraction.

Use Small-Group **>**
Interactions

Show children 10 color tiles. Then write $10 - 5 = 5$ on the board. **I have 10 tiles altogether. If I take away 5 of them, how many will be left?** *(5)* **That's right, there will be 5 tiles left.** Demonstrate the process. **Now let's see you do the same thing.**

Divide the class into pairs and distribute an index card and 10 color tiles to each pair. Have children use their tiles to illustrate the number sentence written on their card. Encourage them to describe what they did. For example: "I had 10 tiles. I took away 2 of them. 8 tiles are left."

Problem-Solving Applications:
Walk, Swim, or Fly

ACCESS CONTENT

Objective Review and apply key concepts, skills, and strategies
learned in this and previous chapters.

Materials *(per pair)* Cup; combination of 8–10 pennies and dimes

ESL Strategies   *Use before* **LEARN**   ⏱ 10–15 MIN

Use Demonstration ➤ Display 3 pennies and 5 dimes. **I see 8 coins in all. 3 of the coins are
pennies.** On the board write 8 − 3. **If I want to find out how many dimes
there are, I need to write a subtraction sentence.** Explain that the 8
represents the total number of coins. To find the number of dimes, you need to
subtract the number of pennies from the total number of coins. Point to the 3
and say: **This is the number of pennies. Let's complete the sentence.** Write
= 5 after the 3. **8 minus 3 equals 5. There are 5 dimes.** Count the dimes
aloud to check the answer. Repeat the process, using other combinations of 8.

Use Small-Group ➤ Write the following question on the board: "How many pennies do you
Interactions have?" Read the question aloud. Empty a cup containing 3 pennies and 3
dimes. Count all of the coins and say: **I have 6 coins, so I will write 6.** Tell
children that in order to find out how many pennies there are, you can
subtract the number of dimes from the total number of coins. **Let's count the
number of dimes together. 1, 2, 3. I have 3 dimes, so I will write − 3 after
the 6. Now what I have written says 6 minus 3.** Take the three dimes from
the total and say: **Now I will count my pennies. I have 3 pennies.** Write
= 3 and read the number sentence together: "**6 − 3 = 3.**"

Provide each pair with a cup filled with 8–10 pennies and dimes. Invite children
in each pair to write their own subtraction sentence answering the question on
the board. Then have them explain in their own words what they did.

Counting Sets of 10

12-1

ACCESS CONTENT

Objective Count groups of 10, up to 10 tens, and write how many.

Materials *(per child)* 10 × 10 square grid; crayons

Vocabulary Count by 10s

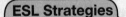 **ESL Strategies** ➤ *Use before* **LEARN** 🕐 10–15 MIN

I HAVE COLORED
10 SQUARES BLUE.

Use Graphic Organizers ➤ Draw a 10 × 10 square grid on the board or chart paper. Then distribute a 10 ×10 square grid to each child. **We all have the same page: a grid showing lots of boxes. I'm going to color in 10 squares in the top row, using blue.** Count off each square as you color it. Then say: **I have colored 10 squares blue.** Invite children to color 10 squares in blue on the top row of their grids. Check each child's grid to make sure that he or she has correctly colored 10 squares. **We have each counted and colored 10 squares blue. There are 10 blue squares in all on each of our grids.**

Tell children that you are going to color 10 more squares, this time using red. Point to the second row and count the 10 squares in it aloud, from 11 to 20, before coloring them in. Instruct children to do the same on their own charts. Then have children count along with you, from 1 to 20. **How many blue squares are there?** *(10)* **How many red squares are there?** *(10)* **How many colored squares are there altogether?** *(20)* Continue in this manner, using different colors for numbers 21–30, 31–40, 41–50, 51–60, 61–70, 71–80, 81–90, and 91–100. Instruct children to focus on the number of squares just colored (always 10) and the total number of squares colored thus far (the previous total plus 10 more).

When everyone has completed coloring the 100 squares, row by row, show children how to count by 10s, row by row. Then have children count by 10s with you in unison: **"10, 20, 30, 40, 50, 60, 70, 80, 90, 100."** Finally, have volunteers count to 100 by 10s, with help from their classmates as needed.

Numbers to 100

ACCESS CONTENT

USE WITH LESSON 12-2

Objective Count and write numbers to 100 on the hundred chart.

Materials Hundred Chart (Teaching Tool 42)

Vocabulary Hundred chart

ESL Strategies

Use before **LEARN**

 10–15 MIN

Use Gestures ➤ Show children the <u>hundred chart</u>. Explain that there are 100 numbers on this chart and that they are all in order. **Let's see how the numbers are ordered.**

Point to the top, left-hand square on the chart. **This is the top left corner of the chart. What number is in this first square?** *(1)*

1	2	3	4	5	6	7	8	9	10
11	12	13	14	15	16	17	18	19	20
21	22	23	24	25	26	27	28	29	30
31	32	33	34	35	36	37	38	39	40
41	42	43	44	45	46	47	48	49	50
51	52	53	54	55	56	57	58	59	60
61	62	63	64	65	66	67	68	69	70
71	72	73	74	75	76	77	78	79	80
81	82	83	84	85	86	87	88	89	90
91	92	93	94	95	96	97	98	99	100

Gesture with your finger as you say: **Now I'll move my finger to the right, to the next square. What number is this?** *(2)* As you move your finger into the next box ask: **Who can tell me what number is to the right of the number 2?** *(3)* Continue in this manner until you reach the end of the row. Explain that you will now need to return to the left side of the chart to find the number 11. Point out that 11 is 1 square down from the number 1.

Count from 1 to 10 again, pointing to each square as you count. When you get to 10, tell children that you will swing your finger back to the left side of the chart to continue counting.

Continue counting the numbers on the entire chart with children, pointing to each number as you proceed. Invite volunteers to come to the chart and count aloud. Encourage them to use directional words and phrases, such as "to the right," "across the row," "down one row," and "in the next square."

Counting Large Quantities

ACCESS CONTENT

Objective Count groups of 10 and count on to find how many.

Vocabulary *(per pair)* 21–35 two-color counters

ESL Strategies *Use before* **LEARN** ⏱ 10–15 MIN

Use ➤
Demonstration
Remind children that they have used their ten-frames to help them count greater numbers. Tell them they will now learn how to count greater numbers without using their ten-frames. Display 33 counters. **Here are some counters. What are some ways that I can count them?** *(Accept all reasonable responses.)* **I can count them by 1s.** Demonstrate by counting each counter one at a time. **So, when I count my counters by 1s, I find out that I have 33 counters in all. Could I also count my counters by 10s?** *(Yes)*

Okay, now I will count my counters by tens. Who can tell me what I need to do first? *(Make groups of 10.)* After you have counted out, and separated out, 3 groups of 10, say: **I don't have enough counters to make another group of 10, so I will keep these 3 leftovers separate.** Have 3 volunteers count each group of 10 to verify that there are, indeed, 10 counters in each group. Then point to each group as you count the 3 groups by 10s: **10, 20, 30. I have 30 counters here. Now I will count the leftovers by 1s: 31, 32, 33. So, I do have 33 counters in all.** Explain that whether you count by 1s or count by 10s (and then count any leftovers), the number of counters is the same. **Why would you want to count a large number of things by 10s rather than by 1s?** *(Because it's faster)*

Paraphrase Ideas ➤
Divide the class into pairs. Provide each pair of children with 21–35 counters and have them count their counters by 10s. As you visit each pair, ask children to describe what they are doing. Encourage children to use complete sentences, but accept gestures and phrases as well.

2s, 5s, and 10s on the Hundred Chart

ACCESS CONTENT

Objective Use a hundred chart to count by 2s, 5s, and 10s.

Materials Chart paper; green felt-tip marker or small green counter; self-stick notes; *(per child)* Hundred Chart (Teaching Tool 42)

Vocabulary Count by 2s, count by 5s, count by 10s

ESL Strategies *Use before* **LEARN** ⏱ 10–15 MIN

Use Gestures ➤
Draw a hundred chart on chart paper. Then provide each child with a hundred chart of his or her own. Show children a small item, such as a green felt-tip marker, and tell children that you are going to pretend that it is a leap frog. Explain that this leap frog hops only by 2s. Use self-stick notes to cover

all of the odd numbers between 1 and 19 (1, 3, 5, 7, and so on). Next, place the marker on the number 2. **Remember, our leap frog can hop only by 2s. He is on 2 right now. So what is the next number that our frog can hop to?** *(4)* Point to the number 4. **If I skip count, or <u>count by 2s</u>, the next number the frog can land on is number 4.** Demonstrate with the marker as you "hop" to number 4. Then say: **What is the next number that our little leap frog can hop to?** *(6)* **That's right, number 6.** Continue in this manner until you reach the number 20. Repeat the process and have children follow along using their fingers as they count by 2s.

Then have the frog "hop" as you <u>count by 5s</u> and <u>count by 10s</u>.

Use Small-Group ➤ Interactions Have pairs work together to count by 2s, starting with 0. As you visit each pair, ask children to show you how to count by 2s. Then have children repeat the process, counting by 5s and then by 10s.

Counting by 2s, 5s, and 10s

USE WITH LESSON 12-5

ACCESS CONTENT

Objective Count groups by 2s, 5s, and 10s to find the total number.

Materials 20 pencils (or pens)

Vocabulary Count by 2s, count by 5s, count by 10s

ESL Strategies *Use before* **LEARN** ⏱ 10 MIN

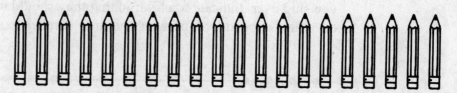

Use Real Objects ➤ Display 20 pencils (or pens). **Let's <u>count</u> these pencils <u>by 2s</u>.** Group the pencils by 2s. Then count the pencils aloud by 2s. Repeat the process, this time having children join in with you. Write the total number of pencils on the board. **Now, let's <u>count</u> these pencils <u>by 5s</u>. What do we need to do first?** *(Put the pencils in groups of 5)*. **That's right, we need to put the pencils in groups of 5.** Count by 5s as you point to each group of pencils. Again, have children count along with you: **"5, 10, 15, 20." How many pencils are there?** *(20)* **Did the number of pencils change when we counted them by 5s?** *(No)* **That's right, there are still 20 pencils. Now let's <u>count</u> these same pencils <u>by 10s</u>.** Model putting the pencils into two groups of 10 each. Have 2 volunteers count the pencils to verify that there are, in fact, 10 pencils in each group. Then count the pencils by 10s. **How many pencils are there?** *(20)* **Did the total number pencils change?** *(No)* Explain that the number of pencils remains whether you count by 2s, count by 5s, or count by 10s.

Problem Solving Strategy: Look for a Pattern

ACCESS CONTENT

Objective Solve problems by identifying and extending number patterns based on counting by 2s, 5s, and 10s.

Materials *(per pair)* 0–20 number line; cup filled with 10 two-color counters; slips of paper or self-stick notes

| **ESL Strategies** | ***Use before*** **LEARN** | 10–15 MIN |

Use Manipulatives ➤ Draw a number line from 0 to 20 on the board. Distribute a 0–20 number line and a cup filled with 10 counters to each pair of children. Remind children that a number line can be used to count numbers one at a time: 0, 1, 2, 3, and so on.

Remind children that they have also learned other ways to count. Ask children to talk about some of these ways. You may need to remind children that they can also count objects in groups, such as when they count something by 2s. Point to the number line on the board and demonstrate counting by 2s: **0, 2, 4, 6, 8, 10, 12, 14, 16, 18, 20.** Count again as you point to the numbers and have children count aloud with you. Explain that you skipped over a number each time you counted. Invite children to share some of the numbers that you skipped over. Then count once more, this time taping a piece of paper over each number that you skip over. Indicate to children that they should use their counters to cover the skipped-over numbers on their number lines. (See illustration.)

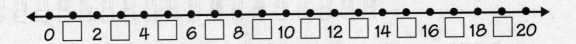

Remind children that a pattern is something that repeats over and over again. **Can you see a pattern here?** *(Yes, the numbers are skipping by 2s like this: say a number, skip a number; say a number, skip a number; say a number, skip a number—over and over again.)* Repeat the process as children skip count by 5s and 10s.

Problem-Solving Applications: Nature Walk

ACCESS CONTENT; EXTEND LANGUAGE

Objective Review and apply key concepts, skills, and strategies learned in this and previous chapters.

Materials *(per pair)* Chart paper; markers

Use Total Physical Response ➤ Invite 3 children to stand in a row facing the class. Tell Child A to hold his or her 10 fingers "high in the air." Point to each finger as you model counting it as part of a set of 10. Then ask: **How many fingers does (Child A) have?** *(10)* **That's right.** Repeat the process with each child. Explain that you can find out how many fingers the 3 children have altogether by counting by 10s. Model counting the fingers by 10s as you tap each of the 3 children on the shoulder, one at a time, in left to right sequence: **10, 20, 30. These 3 children have 30 fingers in all.** Invite another child to come to the front of the class. **How many fingers does (Child D) have? Let's count them together: "1, 2, 3, 4, 5, 6, 7, 8, 9, 10." Now, how many fingers do these 4 children have altogether?** Model counting all 4 children's fingers by 10s as you gesture to each child in turn. Repeat this process until you have counted 10 children's fingers to 100.

Provide each pair of children with a large piece of chart paper and a marker. Tell children to choose one of the following numbers: 20, 30, 40, 50, 60. Have them write the number at the bottom of their paper. Then tell children to trace their fingers in groups of 10 to illustrate the number that they chose. Have them circle each group of 10. Then invite them to describe the total number of fingers they traced and to tell how many groups of ten they have in all.